On
Music

"This is a great introduction to the philosophy of music—accessible yet sophisticated and comprehensive—that is distinguished by the range and variety of musical examples with which it illustrates the issues."
—Stephen Davies, University of Auckland

"Ted Gracyk's *On Music* is the best brief overview there is of the core philosophical questions about music. It's a great introduction to philosophy for music-lovers, packed with a wide range of pertinent musical examples, from birdsong to bluegrass, Romanticism to ragas. And for those already familiar with the questions it is a rare opportunity to see how a philosopher at the top of his game sees one set of answers hanging together—a unified vision of the nature and value of music."
—Andrew Kania, Trinity University

After earning a Ph.D. in Philosophy from the University of California, Davis, **Theodore Gracyk** has spent the bulk of his teaching career in Minnesota. Having published extensively in philosophy of art, philosophy of music, and the history of aesthetics, he became co-editor of *The Journal of Aesthetics and Art Criticism* in 2013. His *Rhythm and Noise: An Aesthetics of Rock* (1996) was a groundbreaking exploration of the aesthetics of popular music. He is the co-editor, with Andrew Kania, of the *Routledge Companion to Philosophy and Music* (2011).

Praise for the series

'. . . allows a space for distinguished thinkers to write about their passions.'
The Philosophers' Magazine

'. . . deserve high praise.'
Boyd Tonkin, The Independent (UK)

'This is clearly an important series. I look forward to receiving future volumes.'
Frank Kermode, author of Shakespeare's Language

'both rigorous and accessible.'
Humanist News

'the series looks superb.'
Quentin Skinner

'. . . an excellent and beautiful series.'
Ben Rogers, author of A.J. Ayer: A Life

'Routledge's Thinking in Action series is the theory junkie's answer to the eminently pocketable Penguin 60s series.'
Mute Magazine (UK)

'Routledge's new series, Thinking in Action, brings philosophers to our aid. . . .'
The Evening Standard (UK)

'. . . a welcome series by Routledge.'
Bulletin of Science, Technology and Society (Can)

'Routledge's innovative new "Thinking in Action" series takes the concept of philosophy a step further.'
The Bookwatch

THEODORE GRACYK

On
Music

Routledge
Taylor & Francis Group
NEW YORK AND LONDON

First published 2013
by Routledge
711 Third Avenue, New York, NY 10017

Simultaneously published in the UK
by Routledge
2 Park Square, Milton Park, Abingdon, Oxon OX14 4RN

Routledge is an imprint of the Taylor & Francis Group, an informa business

© 2013 Taylor & Francis

Library of Congress Cataloging in Publication Data
Gracyk, Theodore.
    On music/by Theodore Gracyk.
    pages cm.—(Thinking in action)
    Includes bibliographical references and index.
    1. Music—Philosophy and aesthetics.   I. Title.
    ML3800.G6607 2013
    781.1′7—dc23
    2012045261

ISBN: 978-0-415-80777-7 (hbk)
ISBN: 978-0-415-80778-4 (pbk)
ISBN: 978-0-203-14577-7 (ebk)

Typeset in Joanna and DIN
by Florence Production Ltd, Stoodleigh, Devon, UK

For Arnold Johanson

What is your aim in philosophy?—To show the fly the way out of the fly-bottle.
(Ludwig Wittgenstein)

This short book is intended for readers who think that music is something very important, but who want to get beyond the usual clichés in thinking about why that is. My inspiration is Friedrich Nietzsche's much-quoted remark, "Without music, life would be a mistake." Nietzsche wrote that aphorism in the late nineteenth century, but the same point had already been made by Protarchus in the fourth century BCE.

I begin, in Chapter 1, with the question of what music is. Sound, obviously. (But is it really so obvious? Chapter 1 observes that many ancient and medieval writers thought otherwise.) Besides sound, what else is required? And, whatever it is, is it merely human life that would be a mistake without it? The remaining chapters address, from several angles, whether Nietzsche is correct. Is there anything that music does for us that cannot be done in its absence? For if something else can take its place, then it cannot be true that life without music is a mistake.

The Thinking in Action series is intended for a general, non-specialist audience. If you have a degree in philosophy, you may not find anything especially new or challenging in the second and third chapters of this book. Advanced degree in musicology? Ditto. You might prefer *The Routledge Companion to Philosophy and Music*, which I co-edited with Andrew Kania. The experience of editing the *Companion* led directly to this book. Invited to distill what I learned from that King Kong of a project into 40,000 words, I have selected four topics. Roughly, in order, those topics are music's relationships to art, language, emotion, and spirituality. They were chosen less because they interest contemporary philosophers than because they are topics that people often bring up when talking about music. That isn't to say that this book is something less than "real" philosophy. It is to say, instead, that the philosophizing arises out of several perennially interesting topics. My orientation is captured by Ludwig Wittgenstein's suggestion, "The work of the philosopher consists in assembling reminders for a particular purpose." My purpose is to show that some very common assumptions about music are confused and misleading. Our listening is informed by competing folk-theories about music. It is also informed by centuries of philosophical speculation about music. As a result, a lot of what we believe about music is very doubtful. Again, in the spirit of Wittgenstein, the goal here is to identify the sources of these errors and, by locating them, to become less likely to fall back into them. In many cases, the way forward requires us to become aware of how various words and phrases are used at cross-purposes in different contexts. Clarity is also achieved by recognizing that very small descriptive differences can have significant implications, as when the third chapter discusses the difference between describing music as expressing emotions and its being expressive of them.

I should also highlight some strategies that I employ in this book. First, when I provide an example, I generally provide at least two. One is usually drawn from "high" culture and the other from "popular" culture. The point of this strategy is to offer ongoing reminders that I am discussing music generally and not just "classical" or "art" music. Second, I hope that my readers will endorse my decision to do without the apparatus of footnotes and textual citations. When I employ quotation or close paraphrase, I identify my source by author. Each author has a corresponding entry in the list of references at the back. In the age of easy Internet searches, the precise sources of my quotations are easily discovered from that minimal information.

Finally, I want to make it clear that I make no claim about saying anything original here. Philosophers have discussed the essence and value of music since the beginning of the recorded Western tradition. Music interested both Plato and Aristotle. Significantly, theorizing about the nature of music also dates back to recorded beginnings of the philosophical traditions of India and China. Viewed against this long tradition, my ideas are necessarily derivative. In particular, everything I say and think about music owes an extraordinary debt to Stephen Davies, Kathleen Higgins, Peter Kivy, Lee B. Brown, Malcolm Budd, Jenefer Robinson, and Robert Stecker. At crucial junctures, my thinking was redirected by professional and personal encounters with Joel Rudinow, Crispin Sartwell, Alex Neill, Jeanette Bicknell, Cynthia Grund, Stan Godlovitch, Denis Dutton, Andrew Kania, and Tiger Roholt. Stephen Davies and Andrew Kania read the manuscript as it neared completion and gave me many helpful suggestions for improvement. And many thanks go to Andrew Beck at Routledge for encouraging me to write this book.

SUMMARY

Is all music art? I contend that it is. Chapter 1 examines what is required to secure that status for music. While this starting point might not be the most obvious place to begin an analysis of music, it invites me to contrast competing ideas about the essential nature of music. In order to establish that music is more than musically organized sound, I organize the chapter around the position that songbirds do not produce music. Their songs are not music for the same reason that "the music of the spheres" does not fall within the scope of the modern concept of music. Employing a common definition of "culture," they lack the cultural dimension that secures art status for music.

Chapter 2 builds on the idea that musical style embeds every piece of music in a network of historical forces and compositional choices. There is a significant body of instrumental music that is regarded as special because it is "pure" music— music that should be understood and appreciated without employing any non-musical ideas. However, informed listening requires the acquisition of language that furnishes appropriate conceptual guidelines. But once we agree that there is more to music listening than meets the ear, we have no basis for singling out some music as "pure" in the intended sense.

Chapter 3 takes up the common view that music is inherently linked to the expression of emotion. I examine several theories of musical expression and conclude that none of these theories applies to all music.

Chapter 4 examines the widespread conviction that music provides spiritual insight. I examine the views of Arthur Schopenhauer and argue that his position conflicts with my conclusions in earlier chapters. It is another variation of the mistaken view that the imposition of ideas interferes with aesthetic response. Additionally, I suggest that the aesthetic property of sublimity is a neglected vehicle for spiritual insight through music.

One

Adieu! adieu! thy plaintive anthem fades
Past the near meadows, over the still stream,
Up the hill-side; and now 'tis buried deep
In the next valley-glades:
Was it a vision, or a waking dream?
Fled is that music—do I wake or sleep?
(John Keats, "Ode to the
Nightingale")

This book is a philosophical examination of the nature of music. More specifically, it examines puzzles generated by its status as art. Here is one of those puzzles. Our brains appear to be hard-wired for music. But when we're hard-wired to engage in an activity—eating, sleeping, breathing—we tend to regard it as an animal response. These activities seem to be the very opposite of art. If Miles Davis's Kind of Blue album consisted of the sound of his breathing, rather than the sound of his trumpet, why would it be an artistic achievement?

Perhaps a hard-wired activity is transformed into art when it is an exceptionally fine example of something that everyone does, but which few do well. Perhaps Kind of Blue is art in the way that the Taj Mahal is a work of art. Compared with most other buildings in a world of cookie-cutter construction, the Taj Mahal is a breathtaking achievement. In this evaluative sense of "art," few products of human activity rise to the level of being art. The drawings that my children made at school were displayed on our refrigerator, but they weren't art in the evaluative sense of the term. In contrast, Georges Seurat's magnificent painting *A Sunday on La Grande Jatte*, at the Chicago Art Institute, is a work of art. Three blocks away, the pizza at Chicago's Exchequer Pub also counts as art, as compared with the stuff sold by the major pizza delivery chains. Notice, however, that a comparative standard generates its own difficulty. If music is art only when it exceeds ordinary standards, then we must say that very little music is art. But this rubs me wrong. From *Kind of Blue* to the shamisen accompaniment of bunraku (Japanese puppet theater) to the soundtrack of a commercial video game, I think that all music is art.

So which is it? Should we think that music, as an art, is a universal human activity that ranges from the trivial to the magnificent? From the song "Old McDonald Had a Farm" to Olivier Messiaen's *Quatuor pour la fin du temps* (Quartet for the End of Time)? From downloaded ring tones on mobile telephones to the raga Marwa, one of the most challenging pieces in the classical tradition of northern India? That seems awfully generous. If it is too generous, should we look for the difference that divides music into two great camps, the artistic and the rest? This chapter will consider these competing proposals. I contend that we should err on the side of generosity.

I. BIRDS

Philosophers often attack a problem sideways. Instead of addressing a problem directly, philosophers sometimes explore a related topic as a neutral territory for clarifying the issues and making important distinctions. Then we see how these ideas apply to the main topic of interest. For example, in pursuing the topic of virtue, Socrates asks us to think about different species of bees. In that spirit, I want to discuss music by thinking about birds. Geese and nightingales, for starters.

I was born and raised near the Pacific Ocean. There are plenty of sea gulls but there are no geese. As an adult, I moved near the geographical center of North America. Now, nearly three decades later, I still respond to the annual migration of snow geese as a novelty. My wife and I take great delight in the fluid ribbons of geese undulating across the sky. We often hear the distinctive honking of the geese before we see them, and this makes us look to the sky for them. Like the red leaves of autumn and the green buds of spring, their honking is a transitory feature of nature associated with specific seasons of the year.

Why do the geese honk? I have always supposed that they are "talking" to one another. Not real talking, of course. Not language use, in which a vocabulary is combined with grammatical rules to convey complex thoughts. We have no reason to think that one goose calls out to another, "That was a good dinner last night." All the same, the geese are communicating with sound. The related point is that I would never say that geese sing, and I would never say that they make music. In this respect, geese are like crows and owls. They are very different from nightingales and other songbirds. (Ironically, media software used for digital music has been named both Songbird and Nightingale, but I can find no evidence of media software named for geese and owls.) However, my exclusion of the hooting, screeching, and "chittering" of the great horned owls that sometimes perch in the pine tree in my backyard may be nothing more than a cultural prejudice. Many medieval writers praised the owl's singing for its simplicity and solemnity, and recommended it to the clergy as a model for human song. In particular, the owl's hooting was recommended as a better model than the flashy and trivial singing of the two species of nightingales.

Does it really matter whether owls and geese sing? Until the nineteenth century, European culture regarded singing as one of the paradigms of music making. Where there is singing, there is music. Therefore, if owls and nightingales sing, they make music, and *Homo sapiens* are not the only animals who make music. Unfortunately, this idea has its down side. If birds make music by virtue of singing, then there is nothing especially *human* about music making. Music making is no more human than is seeing, eating food, or developing arthritic hips—three things that were also true of my family's aging Labrador retriever. If some birds sing, then we humans make music because we are musical animals, alongside other musical animals, and it is an error to suppose that all music is art. Since I want to deny that implication, I am going to argue that birds don't sing or make music—at least not in the sense of "sing" and "music" that is characteristically human. (I remain an agnostic about whale songs.)

While it easy to deny that geese and crows are musical, there is a very old tradition of ascribing song to nightingales. In Hesiod's account of the oldest of Aesop's fables, a hawk describes a nightingale as a singer. In the nineteenth century, Europe's most popular singer was Jenny Lind, "the Swedish Nightingale." (Who would have paid to hear the Swedish Goose, or the Swedish Owl?) A century later, Vera Lynn's recording of the song "A Nightingale Sang in Berkeley Square" was heard throughout England in the fall of 1940. The German air force was unleashing a massive bombing campaign on London and other English cities. Each morning the citizens of England awaited word on the previous night's devastation. In the wake of the destruction of whole neighborhoods and of much-loved London landmarks, the song's references to Mayfair and dining at the Ritz served as a potent reminder of what the Germans sought to obliterate. After the war, "A Nightingale Sang in Berkeley Square" became something of a jazz standard, eventually finding a new audience in the twenty-first century when it was covered by Rod Stewart, a bluesy rock and roll singer turned crooner.

Because male nightingales sing, common sense seems to dictate that some birds make music. All too often, however, "common sense" encodes cultural prejudices. If it is common sense to attribute music to songbirds, there is also an opposing, equally ancient tradition of explaining why there is more here than meets the ear. One of the oldest philosophical distinctions is Plato's opposition of the worlds of becoming and of being, of what we perceive and what is. A good magician can make it appear that an event happens when it does not happen: an elephant seems to vanish when its position is unchanged. A pool of water can be an optical illusion generated by heat waves. Similarly, something can sound musical without being music. Philosophy of music was hotly debated in antiquity and the Middle Ages, and Guido d'Arezzo's eleventh-century criterion was well known and often cited:

> Great is the gap between musicians and singers,
> The latter talk about what music comprises,
> While the former understand these things.
> For he who does what he does not understand is termed
>   a beast.

Like honking geese and hooting owls, nightingales were classified as beasts lacking rational understanding. Therefore their songs are not music. Updating this tradition, I argue that birdsong sounds musical, yet it is not music. After that, I will unpack the implications of that distinction for human music making.

II. MUSIC AND THE MUSICAL

Contrary to Jean-Philippe Rameau, the verdict of the ear is not always right concerning music. A nightingale's song is highly musical, but it is a mistake to suppose everything musical is music. By way of analogy, I have occasionally attributed "piggy" behavior to people. As evidenced by George Harrison's delightful song, "Piggies," I am not the only one. A mild example of human pigginess is the dinner guest who takes a third helping of dessert before others have had seconds. Despite the label, it is a mistake to infer that a piggy person is a genuine member of the species *Sus scrofa domestica*, that is, the domesticated pig. A parallel distinction arises with the musical and music.

For example, rhythm is a core feature of most music. By definition, a rhythm is a pattern of recurring stresses within a pulse. Experiments with human hearing demonstrate that we tend to perceive rhythmic differentiation when there is merely a regular pulse. A machine that produces a steady, regular pulse of sound at uniform volume—the clicking of a ratchet wheel, for example—is *perceived* as falling into regular groupings of two or three even when there is no stress pattern. This human tendency to hear a stress pattern where there isn't one is an interesting fact about our instinctive imposition of grouping onto data. However, the psychological tendency to impose a grouping, and thus to hear what isn't there, is no reason to say that the ratchet wheel has a rhythm. Vision is subject to parallel tendencies. Stare at an image of black, teal, and yellow stripes for half a minute and then look at blank white paper. You will see a visual after-image of red, white, and blue. Hopefully, you'll realize that what you "see" is not really there. By extension, the psychological tendency to *hear* warbling as singing is no evidence that there *is* singing taking place when a nightingale "sings."

Ornithologists contend that bird songs have two functions that separate them from other communications by birds. In some cases, they indicate that the singing bird already occupies that territory. In other cases, he is providing evidence that he will be a splendid mate. As with some human communication, an ordinary task is made special by adding musical qualities. What are these qualities? Rather obviously, "songs" require a temporal unfolding of distinctively pitched tones. In short, songs have melodies. The songs of two species of songbirds differ melodically; different species produce distinctive patterns of pitched sounds. Birds also exploit the musical parameters of rhythm and timbre. For example, different birds favor different tempos. Finally, different species of birds produce different timbres or qualities of sound. Pitch and rhythm aside, a wood thrush has a flute-like quality that no goose can produce. Thanks to an avid group of bird lovers who film songbirds and post the footage, everyone with an Internet connection has access to numerous samples of bird "music." After a bit of attentive listening, most people can distinguish the song of the canyon wren from a wood thrush as readily as they can distinguish a slow Baroque flute solo from a passage of rapid Cajun fiddling. Within each species, the songs of individual birds also differ, just as Glenn Gould's 1955 interpretation of J.S. Bach's *Goldberg Variations* differs from Murray Perahia's, just as Stewart's reading of "Berkeley Square" differs from Lynn's.

After reading several ornithologists on the topic of why birds sing, I listened to a few hours of birdsong. I concentrated on songs that birders value highly, such as the skylark and the mistle thrush. What did I hear? Many birds exploit rhythm and pitch in ways that are undeniably musical. Like us, songbirds are attuned to the way that two sounds with the same timbre can be differentiated in pitch, duration, or both. However, geese do that, too, and yet they do not sound musical. Nightingales and skylarks can do what geese never do, which is to arrange a string of sounds with various frequencies into a distinctive, melodic-sounding pattern.

Although nightingales produce "melodies," it does not yet follow that they produce music. The presence of a few common elements does not establish that two kinds of things are really the same thing. In addition to locating features that are common to all music, we need to know that this combination is unique, occurring in nothing but music. Here, we encounter the central problem with the thesis that bird "singing" is music. The features noted so far (pitch and rhythm and timbre) are manipulated in human vocalizing that is not music. For example, a rising pitch at the end of a sentence turns it into a question. Notice the difference when reading the first two lines of William Shakespeare's "Sonnet 18":

> Shall I compare thee to a summer's day?
> Thou art more lovely and more temperate

Now, I invite you to read it aloud twice, adding a question mark to the second line. You will produce a sequence of sounds with a distinctive rhythm and with a repeating pitch pattern. Although the result is musical, poems that string together questions are not music. Yet they have precisely as much claim to being music as a nightingale's song.

I admit that using the opening lines of Shakespeare's "Sonnet 18" is a weak example. Poems are themselves sometimes classified as music. However, there is plenty of ordinary spoken prose that reinforces the point that a few shared features are insufficient to establish that what is musical is also music. Some languages employ pitch to distinguish different words that are otherwise pronounced the same way. Furthermore, spoken language often takes on a distinct rhythm. In languages with sing-song intonation, such as Swedish, and in those with pitch-sensitive word differentiation, such as Mandarin Chinese, we will find occasions where spoken prose shares all the features that produce the musicality of a nightingale's song. For example, hearing a Swedish woman reading a bedtime story to a child, I might make a mistake and think that she is singing a rather dull song. Yet my naïve impression is hardly the test of whether she is making music. The test is to ask culturally attuned listeners. Since the residents of Stockholm and Beijing recognize a difference between speaking and singing in their respective languages, the rhythmic arrangement of sounds into patterns of pitch variation is insufficient to define music.

Although not every rhythmic, melodic pattern counts as music, rhythms and frequencies are the pre-cultural bedrock of musical experience. In perceiving them, we perceive objective formal regularities in movements in our environment. When these movements set up regularities in the air, we hear rhythms and sonic frequencies. (There is a normal range for our species. The fact that there is variability between individuals and over a lifetime does not really complicate anything that is said here.) Of course, hearing is not our sole access to the relationships that strike us as musical. Rhythms can be felt, as well, and thus Evelyn Glennie is a virtuoso professional percussionist despite her lack of hearing.

This relationship between movement and sound creates an interesting puzzle. The ancient Greeks realized that distinctive physical movements correlate with distinctive heard sounds—the most famous example is the discovery, supposedly by Pythagoras around twenty-five centuries ago, that plucking strings of doubled and halved lengths produces the same pitch, but an octave apart. Press any white key on a piano, then count up or down seven white keys, and press that one. Unlike any of the intervening keys, it is recognizably the same note. That is the octave, the point at which the same tone is present again. Like humans, many bird species hear the octave and structure pitch sequences around it, which is one reason that their vocalizations seem to us to be songs. Yet that cannot be the whole explanation, because dogs hear octaves, too. However, dogs do not display that capacity in musical barking and howling.

It occurred to Pythagoras's followers that any regularity in movement is naturally consonant or dissonant with any other, depending on whether the rhythms of the waves of movement are synchronized. For the Pythagoreans and for many subsequent thinkers, the obvious conclusion is that there is music wherever there is regular, synchronized movement. Music need not be audible. Looking at the orderly movements of the planets and the stars, they postulated an unheard harmonization of the music of the spheres—the spheres being the invisible structures that hold the planets and stars in the emptiness of the sky. Given a belief in invisible heavenly spheres, unheard music was not exactly a stretch of the imagination. In the resulting tradition, musical sound was merely a small subset of all the music in the world. For example, early in the sixth century, Boethius taught that music produced by instruments and voices, *musica instrumentalis*, is merely one of four kinds of music. The other three, including the *musica mundana*, the music of the heavens, are unheard.

Once you agree that objective synchronized structures of movement explain the harmonies we hear, and mathematical misalignments explain dissonances, it is a short step to agree that the synchronizations *are* the harmonies, and degrees of misalignment *are* degrees of dissonance. Peter Van der Merwe observes that the minor seventh seems more discordant than the minor third, yet they are "about equally discordant in strictly acoustic terms." In the Pythagorean tradition, the ear should not decide what is proper to music, and the ear is in error to regard the minor third as less discordant.

Although I reject it, the idea that sound is merely a symptom of music had profound consequences in Europe. To note one small example, because the interval of the augmented fourth or diminished fifth is inherently unstable, it was more or less banned in Western music. (The prime example is F sharp in the key of C.) However, this tritone interval was occasionally used to disturb audiences when composers wanted to signify evil. As a result, non-Western and folk traditions that embraced the tritone became doubly problematic, as both discordant and as symbolically aligned with evil. Originally called "the devil in music," the interval's presence in blues music may be a vestigial reason for its reputation as "the devil's music." However, blues music has become so common that its "problem" intervals now sound perfectly natural. And who, in the past half-century, hears this interval in the song "Maria" in *West Side Story* and thinks of it as endowed with evil? The ancient resistance to this dissonant interval seems very quaint. As Marin Mersenne observed in the early seventeenth century, there is very little alignment of mathematical proportions and musical agreeableness.

To be fair, it is a cheap shot to dismiss the Pythagorean tradition as erroneous on the grounds that Eric Clapton's guitar playing and *West Side Story* do not disturb the contemporary ear. A genuine traditionalist looks at contemporary musical taste and sees immature, bad taste. Because the Pythagorean equation of music and harmonious motion is based on theory, not practice, it merits a theory-based response. Mine begins with consideration of the parallel relationship between colors and light waves. Our eyes are completely insensitive to wavelengths beyond the narrow range of so-called "visible" light. In normal vision, we perceive a particular color, red, when the eye registers light wavelengths of 630–650 nanometers. Light with lower wavelengths produces other visual colors. These facts invite the following thought experiment. Suppose that an environmental disaster caused humans to stop seeing colors when wavelengths exceed 500 nanometers. This idea is not radical. In fact, many people are relatively insensitive to the distinctiveness of wavelengths at around 445 nanometers, and so cannot distinguish indigo from blue or purple. Some people are highly sensitive to the difference at this point in the spectrum, and see indigo as distinctly as most people see orange as distinct from red and yellow. My thought experiment takes this fact and extends it. Suppose everyone loses sensitivity to the wavelengths that are perceived as the spectrum of yellows, oranges, and reds. In a world where no one sees them, would the Musée d'Orsay in Paris have a set of light meters on hand, in order to allow visitors to detect and appreciate the subtle interplay of the now-invisible colors of the peaches, oranges, and roses in the still-life paintings of Henri Fantin-Latour? Here, I think, we would agree that invisible colors are not colors at all. Nineteenth-century French paintings are based on the art of exhibiting visible color. If we cannot see Fantin-Latour's colors, the paintings might as well be pencil sketches. Furthermore, the historical curiosity of the fact that sound waves were discovered thousands of years before light waves should not be a reason to think that painting is an art of the visible but music is not an art of sound. The major art forms are rooted in the realm of the aesthetic, of the perceivable. Because I am concerned with the art of music, I think it's merely a metaphor to say that "music" is produced by the moons of Mars as they orbit the red planet. In pursuing a characterization of music that recognizes its status as art, I am unwilling to say, in advance of *hearing* the music, that the interval of the augmented fourth is unsuitable for a love song in *West Side Story*. The verdict of the ear is not always right, but it's not irrelevant, either, for we are dealing with an art of sound.

III. CONCERNING "ART"

There is a position, widespread in the contemporary university, that sees a fool's errand in this reference to the art of sound. One objection is that I cannot be engaged in a descriptive project, for there are no neutral facts to investigate and explain. "Art" is a cultural category of European origin. Non-European cultures did not develop an analogous concept. It is therefore inexcusably Eurocentric to think that "our" art of music is to be found elsewhere, except as an imposition of Western culture. Since I am trying to characterize something that holds for both Western and non-Western musics, my project is prescriptive. This objection deserves a response. I grant that Europeans, in the sway of the Pythagoreans, endorsed a definition of music that does not align with the understanding of any other culture. Does it follow that only Europe had music, and on that basis that it is Eurocentric to classify ancient Sanskrit devotional hymns as music? No. Likewise, the peculiarities of European doctrines connecting art and aesthetic achievement are no reason to think that the statue carvers of the Yoruba people of Nigeria and the Chinese poets of the Han dynasty were not concerned with the aesthetic effects of their art.

To advance a somewhat traditional position, I think art is created whenever musical design is guided by aesthetic standards. Granted, these standards vary by time and place. So understood, the aesthetic dimension of art is not a Western construct. Marc Benamou has lived in Java, interviewed musicians who specialize in its native music, and studied the historical records pertaining to Javanese music. His conclusion? "Musicians, who are mostly from the laboring classes, are as intent on aesthetic properties of music as anyone in Java." Skeptics about the universality of aesthetic response might dismiss the relevance of Benamou's finding on the grounds that the musical tradition of the gamelan orchestras is a culturally rarefied enterprise. It may be the case, the skeptic will say, that a concern for musical beauty and music's aesthetic dimension is "very Javanese," but only because Javanese culture has a high art tradition. However, the skeptic's argument assumes an equation of aesthetics and high art that is refuted by field research. In an interesting coincidence, Denis Dutton and Ellen Dissanayake both lived in India and Papua New Guinea and examined art practices in multiple levels of each society. Independently, both concluded that an important pattern emerges when we stop thinking of "art" as the most high-brow of high-brow material—once we stop equating art, fine art, and capital-A "Art." When we attend to what people in various cultures say about the things they make, it becomes perfectly clear that, despite cultural differences, every tribe and society recognizes special spheres of activity in which aesthetic achievement is valued. Humans routinely distinguish between art and the rest of what they produce. (In anthropology, similar points are raised by Alfred Gell.) Another relevant finding is that, for every human group that has a distinct word for music or, as frequently happens, for a broader category that embraces both music and dance, music always falls into this category. By examining the implications of that point in more detail, I believe we can arrive at a relatively inclusive understanding of art that will give us good reason to say that music is essentially art. As a consequence, it follows that the singing of birds is musical, but it is not an art of music.

IV. MUSIC AND CULTURE

I have allowed that birdsong is music in the obvious sense that it is musical. At the same time, I'm saying that being musical is not sufficient to make it music in our modern sense of the term. It is now time for me to explain why my distinction is genuine. What's the difference? What does birdsong lack?

To proceed by way of analogy, consider a friend's interest in the British television program *Top Gear*, which features cars. Suppose he's particularly enthused about the episode that features a Lamborghini Murciélago sports car. I watch for few minutes, then I dismiss it by saying, "It's just two tons of metal, glass, and plastic, hurled down the pavement at high speed.

What's the big deal?" Although my description is literally true, the Murciélago is not simply two tons of material stuff. Appreciating it requires recognition of differences from other sports cars. Its admirers are completely right to respond to me by emphasizing its distinctive design. That includes looking beyond its most obvious features, such as its low profile and unique door design. A knowledgeable appreciation is influenced by the fact that it is a Lamborghini. As such, it reflects that company's history of car design, which is itself a manifestation of a unique tradition of Italian engineering and design. In short, even if one does not admire the functionality of the Murciélago as a very fast vehicle, one should recognize that it is the physical embodiment of a particular culture's exploration of a more general cultural tradition. In short, it does not simply go fast. It embodies a particular cultural tradition.

Precisely the same point holds for music. Like the Murciélago, performances of music are physically embodied manifestations of a culture. More to the point, that is why music is art and birdsong isn't. But bear with me. This argument will take some time to unfold. It turns on a specific understanding of the concept of culture. Like us, birds have complex social relationships and their vocalizations play an important role in their social interactions. However, cultural interaction involves a great deal more than social interaction.

Suppose that a university student enrolls in a course called "Classical Music," a survey of music from the Baroque period until the early twentieth century. The first day, the instructor begins the class by playing a recording of Mstislav Rostropovich performing the Prelude from Bach's Cello Suite No. 1, which is about two minutes of solo cello playing. A student could respond that it's boring, that it's nothing but someone sawing away on a big fiddle. (That's a genuine response to Bach posted on the Internet regarding another Bach piece.) One goal of the music course is to help that student to hear those two minutes of organized sound as the auditory embodiment of a cultural moment. Let me offer two examples of what I have in mind, involving two different cultural moments.

Joseph Haydn came into his own as a composer while in the employment of the Esterházy family, minor nobility of the Austrian empire. Born in 1732, Haydn held the position of Kapellmeister—literally, "master of the chapel" or director of religious music, but in reality general music director. He gave lessons, wrote music, and led both small and large performing groups. The Esterházy family spent summers in eastern Austria and then in later years at their new palace in western Hungary. They employed an orchestra for which Haydn wrote numerous operas and symphonies. One of his most remarkable symphonies is in F sharp minor. Traditionally numbered as his 45th symphony, it has a highly unusual ending. When the fourth movement begins, the rousing up-tempo music seems typical of closing movements of symphonies at this time. The feeling is triumphant. Around the three-minute mark, there is a radical shift. The music stops without any musical resolution. There is silence. Haydn had already provided the audience with an adagio (slow) second movement. Without any prior signal of heading in a fresh direction, the finale now breaks the silence by offering a second adagio. The effect is as if a Lamborghini Murciélago had been designed to cut back to one-third of its speed when it reached 80 miles per hour. Haydn's finale maintains the new, slow pace for about five minutes. As it proceeds, it gets weirder. Each instrument in the orchestra is given a space in which to play a brief solo passage, after which there is no further music from that instrument. At the end, there are two violins, whose music fades away without any sense of completion.

This musical organization is bizarre. (Is this the first genuine bass solo in Western music?) And it is weird in a way that no birdsong is ever weird. It is intentionally designed to fly in the face of the established conventions of its time and place. It embodies the conventions of mid-eighteenth-century music, and then it shatters them.

As traditionally performed, the symphony has a visual dimension, too. As each instrument ends its part in the finale, that musician stands up and walks off the stage. This practice reflects Haydn's original instructions to his orchestra. In an evening performance, the musicians illuminated their scores with candles on their music stands. When their solo passages reached the end, each musician snuffed out his candle, then left. The stage grew darker as it emptied. The standard explanation of this staging is that Haydn and the orchestra had been kept at the remote palace beyond their usual summer duties, and felt like prisoners. Haydn's music and staging enact the silencing of music through departure. It signaled, in other words, that it was time to leave. According to the early biographies of Haydn, Prince Esterházy got the message and told the musicians that they were free to return to Vienna. This story adds a symbolic dimension to the music. The music is not weird for weirdness's sake. It signifies that an employee, a social inferior, is stepping forward as an individual and disrupting the employer, a superior. It is an assertion of individual will in the face of social expectations. It illustrates the capacity of the human mind to exploit culture in order to signal some degree of independence within society. Most strikingly, as Richard Taruskin emphasizes, it makes its point with "pure" music, with instrumental music that has no vocals.

I offer a second example in order to make the point that this play of culture is not a special capacity of "serious" music. Consider the album *Jaco Pastorius*, the first album released by that jazz musician under his own name, signaling his leadership of the music. The opening piece of music is "Donna Lee," a duet for conga and electric bass. In the context of its release in 1976, it was a revelation, demonstrating that the electric bass can serve as the vehicle for a sustained melodic exploration. In a musical culture that regarded electric bass as a rock and roll instrument and acoustic bass as the only proper instrument for jazz, Pastorius kicked off his solo career with a demonstration of how the jazz tradition was depriving itself of a resource. However, a closer listen reveals another dimension. If jazz traditionalists were likely to be snobs about Pastorius's fusion music, they were likely to recognize the music. "Donna Lee" was Pastorius's arrangement of a 1947 recording by the Charlie Parker quintet. A piece of classic bebop, it is a difficult piece that showcases Parker's skills on the alto saxophone. (There is dispute whether Parker composed it; Miles Davis later claimed authorship.) In recording a bass arrangement of it, Pastorius does more than follow Parker's sax. He also captures supporting harmonies supplied by Bud Powell's piano, demonstrating that his bass could supply the musical lines of two instruments. In selecting this piece as the lead track in his solo debut, Pastorius was making it quite clear that he was placing himself in exalted company.

Having made his point about his place in the tradition, Pastorius challenges that tradition in a second way. The next track is not jazz. It is an original song, "Come On, Come Over," sung by the rhythm and blues duo Sam and Dave. In 1976, the only real opportunity to hear Pastorius's music was to purchase the vinyl album, which meant that every listener heard the flow of tracks in the order established by the album. There was no jumping around on YouTube among different tracks by Pastorius. If you wanted to go from "Donna Lee" to the complex jazz harmonics of the third track, "Continuum," you had to physically manipulate the needle to avoid the intervening pop tune. In short, Pastorius sequenced the album to assert the continuity between advanced jazz and popular music in the African-American tradition. I think he's calling attention to the fact that we couldn't have "Donna Lee" and "Continuum" without the cultural bedrock of blues vocals and the African-American call-and-response format. To embrace Charlie Parker and Miles Davis is to embrace Sam and Dave, too.

There is, then, continuity between Haydn's "farewell" symphony, a Lamborghini Murciélago, the Taj Mahal, a poem by John Keats, and the album *Jaco Pastorius*. Apart from whatever else they are, they embody and respond to their particular cultural traditions. I say culture, and not society, because I am calling attention to the transmission of a group's beliefs and values. Culture is more than social interaction. When a male nightingale's song attracts females, there is social communication. Yet it is not a cultural exchange, for the bird's beliefs and values about the standards for female attractiveness were not acquired from the previous generation in the process of learning to sing. When a North American mockingbird learns to imitate the song of the Carolina wren, it does not appropriate wren culture. In contrast, when the Beatles put flourishes of piccolo trumpet into their arrangement of "Penny Lane," they are appropriating from an identifiable aspect of the culture of J. S. Bach. (They mimic the trumpet of *Brandenburg Concerto No. 2*.) By engaging with inherited and appropriated designs, humans can engage with the associated belief and value systems.

Like bees and whales and birds and dogs, humans are social creatures. Social creatures have to communicate among themselves, and sound is a useful medium for communicating. Yet human beings appear to be the only social animals to have culture, in the sense of culture just explained. This conclusion gives us a definition of music that distinguishes it from what is merely musical. Sound patterns are musical when their organization establishes rhythmic or harmonic relationships (or both). Musical patterns are music only if they reflect—and so are intended to be interpreted in light of—cultural expectations about musical structures. By extension, Andrew Kania reminds us, there is also music in the avant-garde practices of Yoko Ono and John Cage, who present sounds that are unmusical but which are intended to be heard in light of these cultural expectations.

The next point in my argument is to explain why this proposal has the additional result that it makes our music into art, and why that makes music an especially interesting kind of art.

V. THE AESTHETIC DIMENSION

Let's backtrack into the history of ideas again. There is an ancient tradition in which the scope of "music" extends to a great deal of non-audible physical activity. I have indicated that I am pursuing the modern understanding of music as a species of organized sound. For nearly 300 years, the modern tradition regarded music as sound that is organized to be pleasing. In the second half of the nineteenth century, the age of Wagner and Brahms, Eduard Hanslick used his position as Vienna's premier music critic to argue that beautiful organization is the key to musical value. However, practice has defeated theory. The modern art movement of the twentieth century has made it clear that beauty is not essential. Quite apart from the high-art tradition, the same point is made by the musical practices of punk rock, heavy metal, and the repetitive dance grooves of club music. A few people continue to dismiss such music as noise and therefore not real music, but I take that to be an imposition of taste rather than a serious position.

Hanslick was a nineteenth-century music critic who became a professor at the University of Vienna. He was, in effect, the first professional musicologist. His prime years coincided with a bitter dispute about the relative value of opera and instrumental music. There is no obvious opposition here. When Haydn was Kapellmeister at the Esterházy court, he composed both operas and symphonies. For his debut recording, Pastorius composed songs and instrumental music. To generalize very broadly about the history of Western music, Haydn's generation was pivotal in the public's acceptance of instrumental music as a focal point of listening. When music lovers think of Beethoven, they do not remember him for his piano settings of Scottish poetry. They recall his symphonies, piano sonatas, and string quartets. But Beethoven's ninth symphony throws a monkey wrench into the mix, because it ends with a choral setting of a poem. It shattered the conventions for symphonic form that had only recently been established by Haydn and Mozart. However, Wagner thought that Beethoven had it right: great music supports singing in a dramatic performance. In short,

Wagner's ideal music is not instrumental music or "music alone," as it's sometimes called. For Wagner, music is best heard in a mixed-media presentation. It belongs in a Gesamtkunstwerk, a synthesis of arts in one art work. (In the twenty-first century, a Gesamtkunstwerk would require a film-maker who writes an original script, directs the acting, edits the film, and then composes the film score.) Wagner wanted music to contribute to powerful art, rather than to remain a pure art. In comparison with music in music drama, music alone is an anemic art form.

Hanslick's defense of pure instrumental music draws loosely from one of the foundational texts of aesthetic theory, Immanuel Kant's Critique of Judgment. Hanslick probably knew it second-hand, since it was then six decades old and no longer the cutting edge of aesthetics. To put his use of Kant into perspective, it would be as if Hubert L. Dreyfus revised his book On the Internet by adding a chapter that draws heavily on philosophical doctrines that emerged around 1950. However, philosophy is a field where a good idea can have staying power. In that spirit, I want to reach back into Hanslick's On the Musically Beautiful in order to extract lines of argument that are seldom noted or discussed. He cautions that we should not make too much of the fact that music functions in a particular way when it is used in song and music drama. To determine what makes music valuable as an art, we must examine pure instrumental music. With opera and song, we cannot tell how much of the success of a particular combination of words and music is due to the impression made by the words, and how much is due to the success of the music. Because we do have pure instrumental music, and because works such as Bach's Goldberg Variations and Well-Tempered Clavier are masterpieces of the art, it follows that music does not need synthesis with other art forms in order to achieve its full potential as art. Combinations of music and other art media can be very powerful, but that tells us nothing significant about the value and potential of the art of composing music. (We will simply set aside, until the next chapter, the question of whether there is really any such thing as music alone or "pure" instrumental music.)

The heart of the Hanslick–Wagner debate is a point about function as a source of value. My kitchen refrigerator has value as the kind of thing that it is because it succeeds in keeping food and beverages reasonably cold. Granted, one could keep a refrigerator after its motor dies, using it as a storage unit with a door. But that is not to value it as a refrigerator any longer. For Wagner, music drama always has a function, and the music is of value by advancing that purpose. For example, Act 3 of Wagner's *Die Meistersinger von Nürnberg* advances German nationalism. Purists, such as Hanslick, say that its success or failure is independent of that purpose, which is incidental to its status as art. Musical pleasure is the only relevant purpose.

I recommend a third path. We can avoid the polarizing "either/or" that pits Wagner against Hanslick by pursuing one of the controlling insights of George Kubler's study of visual form: "every man-made thing arises from a problem as a purposeful solution." The key term is *purposeful*. In Kant's philosophy, the appreciation of art is the appreciation of its *purposefulness*, which is the *appearance* of having being designed. We seem to be naturally sensitive to the presence of purposiveness. Driving through an unfamiliar stretch of countryside, I am attuned to the difference between ordinary clumps of trees and those planted as windbreaks. With a windbreak, the trees are grouped with a regularity that witnesses human intention. This difference can be detected even when we don't know the actual purpose of a purposeful design. Conversely, we can remain indifferent to its actual purpose or real-world consequences when we know what it is. Thus, I might despise Wagner's purpose and still admire *Die Meistersinger*, just as I can admire the Lamborghini Murciélago despite my genuine indifference to fast cars. My reservations about a designer's goals do not stop me from appreciating the human accomplishment embodied in a purposeful design.

This human capacity to compartmentalize—to appreciate purposefulness apart from purpose—explains how it is possible to admire the art of another culture without endorsing its beliefs and values. But of course the same issue arises *within* a culture. If art appreciation is merely a matter of endorsing functional value, then an atheist cannot value George Frideric Handel's *Messiah*. I cannot value the Philip Glass opera *Satyagraha* because I don't endorse the world view shared by Mahatma Gandhi and the teachings of the ancient Hindu text the *Bhagavad Gita*. Yet many atheists admire *Messiah*, and I admire *Die Meistersinger* and *Satyagraha* despite my conviction that their underlying philosophies are a load of nonsense. Alex Neill and Aaron Ridley have tried to account for this kind of compartmentalization. On their account, an atheist can look beyond "the tissue of superstitious falsehoods" supported by great religious music and instead admire "the [artist's] noble aspiration and commitment to a vision," where that vision affirms the human spirit. However, that seems a bit of a cheat, for it offers no basis of admiration to the bitter misanthrope who thinks that the nobility of the human spirit is, like religion, a destructive falsehood. Neill and Ridley's account requires artist and audience to endorse some shared values. But what if they don't?

In pointing to our capacity to appreciate mere purposefulness, Kant identified the core of aesthetic response as a response to the formal appearance of something. By identifying beauty as music's primary value, Hanslick aligned himself with Kant. Unfortunately, he did so in the context of a debate about instrumental music's capacity to communicate emotion. (I engage with that topic in Chapter 3.) Putting that aside for now, we arrive at a new paradox. With *Messiah* and *Die Meistersinger*, many listeners struggle to set aside the ideas in the text in order to admire the art. So music alone, without text, seems to have the strong advantage that there are no ideas to offend and derail us. It has the same aesthetic status as patterns in rugs and wallpaper. There is nothing to get in the way of appreciating it. As long as the rhythms and harmonies are not too unfamiliar, listening to good music is no more complicated than looking at a sunset. Don't think! Just observe and enjoy. To return to one of my own examples, Hanslick would maintain that hearing Charlie Parker play "Donna Lee" is comparable to looking through the shifting colors in a kaleidoscope. Granted, complex music is more complicated and therefore more engaging, but it is culturally aligned with other modes of decorative design.

In summary, pure instrumental music is important as a test case for a particular aesthetic doctrine, according to which a lack of any particular communicative purpose is no obstacle to artistic success. If lack of purpose is no obstacle, then one's disagreement with purpose is no great obstacle, either. For example, there is considerable debate about the message of Dmitri Shostakovich's fifth symphony. There is conflicting evidence about its proper interpretation. After Joseph Stalin disliked a Shostakovich opera, the Soviet newspaper *Pravda* openly warned the composer about his artistic decadence. Reading between the lines, Shostakovich could read it as an official warning that he must reform or die. Shostakovich wrote his fifth symphony in the next few months. The result is either an endorsement of Marxist principles about art, as understood in the Soviet Union at that time, or it is a very subtle expression of resentment and defiance directed against Stalin's treatment of the Russian people. Although I would like it to be the latter, should I withdraw my admiration if we conclusively prove it is the former? If it is an audible kaleidoscope, it does not matter. It succeeds or fails as a musical pattern.

Here, then, is another paradox. Hanslick has not helped matters. Kaleidoscopes are very rarely artworks. If "Donna Lee" and Wagner's operas are like complicated kaleidoscopes, we've downgraded them. Kant was fully aware of this result, warning that his theory placed instrumental music in "the lowest place among the fine arts." So low a place, it might not count as art. Looking at Hanslick's argument, Mark Evan Bonds nails down the problem. If music is art, Hanslick cannot maintain the kaleidoscope analogy. Sensing the problem, Hanslick dodges it by introducing a lot of talk about music's appeal to *Geist*— the human spirit or mind—and on that basis elevates it, placing it among the arts. Instrumental music has a lofty spiritual content that a kaleidoscope pattern lacks. Unfortunately, when Neill and Ridley discuss *Geist* in religious music, it is music with words. Hanslick never explains how this works for instrumental music. If there really are no ideas present in "Donna Lee" and Bach's *Goldberg Variations*, then they do not seem to be art. To slap a technical label on it, an art-for-art's-sake doctrine of autonomous musical beauty trivializes music. On the other hand, if ideas are present, what are they? And won't their presence reintroduce a need to admire the particular communicative purposes of a musical work in order to admire it in a non-trivial way? Can we salvage the idea of appreciating purposefulness?

VI. CULTURE, COMMUNICATION, AND STYLE

When traditional ideas generate a problem, one solution is to backtrack into history. In that spirit, I want to call attention to an interesting passage in Kant's aesthetic theory. It concerns birdsong:

> What do poets praise more highly than the nightingale's enchantingly beautiful song . . . ? And yet we have cases where some jovial innkeeper, unable to find such a songster, played a trick—received with greatest satisfaction [initially]—on the guests staying at his inn to enjoy the country air, by hiding in a bush some roguish youngster who (with a reed or rush in his mouth) knew how to copy that song in a way very similar to nature's. But as soon as one realizes it was all a deception, no one will long endure listening to this song that before he had considered so charming.

Evidently, tourists have always been targets for exploitation. Setting that aside, Kant is making the point that the charm of the audible pattern is not some autonomous beauty. If we know that a pattern is produced by a human, we respond to it as the activity of a human, and aesthetic judgment cannot circumvent this awareness.

Kant's proposal is significant and, more to the point, it ties back to my distinction between society and culture. We are social animals. As such, we are always thinking about the actions of other humans *as* the actions of other humans. I do not want to rely on the findings of developmental psychology, but there is significant evidence that human babies are hard-wired to look for human faces and to listen to human voices.

Without dwelling on developmental psychology, I proceed with the assumption that we are aware of other members of our species in a special way. Encountering human behavior or even signs of human activity, we interpret them as meaningful. That is, we look for meaning.

There is a strictly philosophical argument that arrives at the same conclusion. If our minds did not contain an innate disposition to identify other people and to seek meaning in their actions, then language acquisition would be impossible. After all, we learn a language from exposure to its use. However, that can only occur if we encounter it in use before we understand it as language. (Otherwise, we wouldn't be *learning* it.) Therefore we cannot learn from it, by experience, that it is a source of meaning. Prior to understanding that it is a source of meaning, it cannot seem to be any more meaningful than anything else we encounter. Yet virtually everyone learns to distinguish language use from other patterns, and children become proficient in a native language long before they grasp the significance of any non-human patterns of equal complexity. Since we are constantly bombarded with other streams of patterned information, our early language acquisition demonstrates that we are hard-wired to attend to it differently. We have a special attunement to patterns of human communication. (As portrayed in the film *A Beautiful Mind*, schizophrenia seems to include a tendency to seek these patterns where they do not exist.)

Back to Kant's odd example. The moment I believe that the warbling in the bush is a human imitation of a nightingale rather than a real nightingale, my attitude changes. A human is deceiving me. The charm vanishes. Contrast this case with hearing someone make the very same sounds in a birdsong imitation contest. Understood as functioning solely as a *representation* of a nightingale, the same sounds can be admired. In the case of the deceptive innkeeper, a guest's recognition of the human source reveals the primary function to be deception, which ruins the experience.

The significant point, generalized, is that we should not respond to a pattern as a mere pattern if we believe it reflects human design. Even if we can do so, we should not respond to Bach or Charlie Parker as if it's an audible kaleidoscope. However, one can become interested in a piece of music in much the way that one can take an interest in the kaleidoscope itself, as an artifact or product of human agency. Gregory Currie's summary of this point is insightful:

> An interest in the aesthetics of artifacts is, for those cases where the distinction is a real one, an interest in something that unites both factors [activity and product]: an interest in the product-as-outcome-of-activity. That is why the aesthetic appreciation of nature *as genuinely natural* is so different from the aesthetic appreciation of art.

You might respond that the aesthetic appreciation of nature is very different when it is a sunset rather than a birdsong. A nightingale's song is the product of an activity. Doesn't that put it on the same level as human music?

There is one more step in this analysis, but it makes all the difference. Musical design displays musical style. This point provides a patch for the hole that Bonds identifies in Hanslick's analysis. It connects musical design to *Geist*. Although Hanslick never postulated this connection, he does make the point that there is no stylistically neutral music. Different societies exploit different aspects of possible musical organization. Musical enjoyment requires a trained (*gebildeten*) ear. Hanslick warns that, however "natural" and "organic" it sounds, musical organization always betrays participation in a cultural tradition:

> What we hear a Tyrolean peasant singing, into which seemingly no trace of art penetrates, is artistic music through and through. Of course, the peasant thinks that he is singing off the top of his head. For that to be possible, however, requires centuries of germination.

To see it from another angle, the universality of language does not lead to a homogeneous world language. Following this analogy, Daniel Levitin explains, "Our brains learn a kind of musical grammar that is specific to the music of our culture, just as we learn to speak the language of our culture." A child learns language by learning *a* language, and a child learns music by learning *a* music. Like language, learning a culturally distinct musical grammar embeds an individual in a culture, and therefore, Hanslick recognizes, in a tradition. However, it doesn't follow that a child, humming the theme song of a favorite television program, is consciously aware of those centuries of preparation. A child in Finland can speak fluent Finnish without becoming aware that there are languages besides Finnish. At the same time, every use of the Finnish language carries two levels of activity. There is the immediate use, for some immediate purpose, such as asking for a cookie or refusing to go to bed. But each time, there is an accompanying activity of carrying on with Finnish culture.

Reflecting on his original purposes as a songwriter, John Lennon told Jann Wenner that the Beatles did not set out to make art. They set out to make functional music. Like the blues, it was music with a purpose in ordinary daily life. Although

Lennon doesn't specify, I take it that the purpose was to support dancing. He offers an interesting metaphor. Jazz and the blues are like two kinds of chairs. Jazz musicians design chairs to show off the design. "The blues is better. [Because] it's chairs for sitting on, not chairs for looking at or being appreciated. You sit on that music." The early Beatles music? "[T]hose were our version of the chair. We were building our own chairs, that's all, and they were sort of local chairs." In other words, they did not set out to be appreciated. They were working-class musicians. Yet they developed their own style of "local chairs," a style of pop music that was then imitated by others and which was initially described as Merseybeat— a reference to the local river. Now we think of it as a style of its own. Driving with my wife recently, listening to the Grateful Dead's *American Beauty* album, she remarked on passages in which the harmonies are clearly Beatles-esque. Lennon didn't set out to create a style. Yet his attempt to be practical, to be functional, required the group to arrange their voices (Lennon and Paul McCartney and George Harrison) and instruments to match their practical abilities and their shared sources of musical knowledge as best they could, and a distinctive style emerged. Each engagement with tradition can change the tradition. In perpetuating culture, the culture itself is gradually transformed—or, sometimes, as with the Beatles, rapidly transformed. Fifty years later, it is easy to appreciate the style of their chairs, which is to appreciate how they deviated from what came before. More importantly, to extend Lennon's metaphor, we can appreciate the local quality of that chair even if we don't want a chair for sitting. And then we can appreciate how that local chair became the foundation of an international style that remains active in pop music today.

All music is art, because all music has style, which means that all music engages actively with the tradition that feeds it. The engagement can be affirmative, or it can be resistive. Either way, it's present. The result is that each act of composing or performing music can be significant as an activity even if it has no immediate function that is achieved by that activity. Therefore it is possible to find the play of culture interesting as culturally formed human activity even where there is no interest in the immediate purpose of that activity.

My point about style is not original. Yet it's a crucial insight about art. Paul Crowther takes it further by noting that style is present in multiple levels of activity. Above all, style is present through "the choice of a medium and facility in using it. The fact that an artist has chosen one medium rather than another, is, in itself, an expression of style." Lennon and the other Beatles-to-be chose the medium of pop songs, and then made choices within that choice. Think back to my earlier example of Pastorius and his decision to record "Donna Lee." There is the decision to play jazz, there is the decision to reach back to bebop, a "dead" style, and then there is the facility displayed on the electric bass itself. There are three levels of style here, none of which are obvious choices for a young man to make if he wants to express himself in the United States in the 1970s. Although he had little use for pop music and jazz in his voluminous writings on the philosophy of music, Theodor Adorno makes an importantly related point. It is completely wrong to think that each piece of music brings together form and content, or to think, with Hanslick, that the musical form just *is* the musical content. Every musician inherits a backlog of musical structures. There are large-scale structures (e.g., the classical symphony as a four-movement work), unit structures (e.g., the sonata–allegro structure of the first movement of such a symphony), melody structures (e.g., the arc of the twelve bars of a standard blues), and brief, local structures (e.g., the cadences that Haydn might have used, but did not, to place resolution at the end of the "Farewell" symphony). As music, these designs are merely jumping-off points for musical activity. *These structures are musical materials.* Like Paul McCartney's Höfner bass guitar or Beethoven's Broadwood piano, they are materials to be used and manipulated. Yet neither the selection of the materials nor the outcomes of the manipulations are pre-ordained.

No nightingale will ever select a Höfner bass in order to supply counterpoint to the song of another nightingale. Birds cannot choose their materials and thus their medium. When a nightingale develops a variation in its inherited song, distinguishing it from that of competing birds, it is not like Pastorius's display of a new variation on "Donna Lee." No bird will plan out ways to frustrate the learned expectations of the other birds in order to make a point to them, as Haydn did with Prince Esterházy. You can admire birdsong all you like, but it cannot be admired as culturally purposeful activity. It cannot be admired as art.

Two

An artist . . . must know that to classify is to embalm. Real identity is incompatible with schools and categories, except by mutilation.

(Mark Rothko)

The words are and remain for the music a foreign extra of secondary value, as the effect of the tones is incomparably more powerful, more infallible, and more rapid than that of the words.

(Arthur Schopenhauer)

I. UNSCHOOLED PERCEPTION

Variants of the same joke about music are attributed to several public figures, but it may have originated with Abraham Lincoln. Some years after the fact, Henry Pearson recalled an 1860 speaking engagement by Lincoln. The evening's other attractions included songs from a vocal quartet. When the music concluded, Lincoln put his arm around the shoulders of the quartet leader and said, "Young man, I wish I could sing as well as you. Unfortunately, I know only two tunes. One is 'Old Hundred,' and the other isn't." The obvious point of the joke is self-deprecation. Lincoln used humor as one of several techniques to make a personal connection to voters as he launched his presidential run.

Taken literally, the joke's wording raises many issues. Is it possible to appreciate music if you really know so little about it? What are you experiencing if you can only name one tune? And yet there are many people who think that knowledge about music interferes with the purity of the experience. Within the philosophical tradition popularized by Jean-Jacques Rousseau and Arthur Schopenhauer, the joke isn't a joke. It's advice. Culture perverts rather than enhances the production and reception of music. In the early twentieth century, art critic Clive Bell defended artistic autonomy and recommended that "to appreciate a work of art we need bring with us nothing from life, no knowledge of its ideas and affairs." On Bell's model of response, valid appreciation of the Prelude from J.S. Bach's Cello Suite No. 1 requires perception of "the rightness of its forms." But this perception requires no training. Taken seriously, this know-nothing, "nothing from life" position holds that the imposition of ideas interferes with aesthetic response. Knowing what a musical suite is, and that J.S. Bach's cello suites originated in the eighteenth century, are irrelevant to perception of the music's formal coherence and value. Or worse—such knowledge detracts from appreciation.

Against the view that it is best to come to art without any preconceptions and without imposing any classifying categories, I argue that there is always more to music than meets the ear. There is wisdom in William Nye's jest that Richard Wagner's music is better than it sounds. The line is often attributed to Mark Twain, who popularized it in his autobiography. Twain quotes Nye in order to underscore the important point that there is such a thing as inappropriate or unjustified boredom. A listener may be incapable of being mistaken about being bored. However, it does not follow that the music is boring. To determine that, one must grasp what is salient, and what is not. In Chapter 1, I offered an analogy between listening to the Bach Prelude and viewing film of a Lamborghini Murciélago sports car. My point was to demonstrate the superficiality of uninformed responses to human designs. Musical style embeds every piece of music in a dense web of historical forces and individual compositional choices. Performance practice adds another layer of choice. Therefore, awareness of stylistic and other historical influences is often required in order to be aware of valuable features of the human designs that we perceive.

Additional background knowledge can be required when music is combined with other art media. Suppose that the student who dismisses the Bach cello music as sawing on a big fiddle encounters the same music again when watching the 2002 film *The Pianist*. The student is in no position to ask why this music from the early eighteenth century is given such prominence in the middle of a film about the Second World War, nor to ask why the remainder of the music is that of Polish composer Frédéric Chopin. The student literally cannot formulate the relevant questions about history and culture explored in the film. (For example, does the presence of Bach signal a shared European culture that informs the actions of both the Poles and the Germans? Or is it a reminder of the gap between human behavior and the ideals embodied in Bach's music?) Yet historical and cultural features are objective, real features of things. Someone who cannot think about the cultural location of the Prelude from Cello Suite No. 1 cannot appreciate *The Pianist* as the film that it is.

These examples invite reflection on why anyone should gain a richer appreciation of art, and why there is a tendency to think less of people who are indifferent to good music. In Shakespeare's *Julius Caesar*, Caesar warns Antony that he must not trust Cassius (Act 1, Scene 2). To make his point, Caesar uses the simple report that "he hears no music." In context, Caesar is saying that Cassius does not appreciate the arts. But is this really a reason to be suspicious of anyone? Because of a lack of appreciation of music? That seems unfair. Like so many human capacities, different people are born with different attunements towards music. Some people are preoccupied with it. At the other extreme, some people suffer from congenital amusia—they simply cannot recognize the musicality of musical sound. There is nothing wrong with their hearing; amusia is found in people with perfect hearing. Yet where others perceive beautiful melodies, amusiacs hear annoying, unpatterned noise. In a case study collected by Oliver Sacks, a woman describes her perception of music as, "If you were in my kitchen and threw all the pots and pans on the floor, that's what I hear." Opera sopranos sound "like screaming." Obviously, the problem is not in the ears but rather in the music processing that takes place in the brain. The consequence is a congenital *perceptual* failure. Perhaps Cassius had amusia. In that case, his lack of interest in music cannot be interpreted as indifference to culture.

Because this book is a philosophical investigation and not a study in the neurophysiology of perception, I call attention to amusia in the spirit of Ludwig Wittgenstein's advice: "The work of the philosopher consists in assembling reminders for a particular purpose." My particular purpose is to present a reminder that, whatever else it is, listeners do not hear music as the music that it is unless they perceive it with understanding. I suspect that no music lover wishes to develop amusia. But if not, why do so many music lovers endorse a partial amusia? For that is the result when listening is not informed by appropriate descriptions and concepts.

The issue of what and how much listeners ought to know is historically connected to the ideal of pure instrumental music. A lot of Bach's instrumental music, such as the Prelude from the Cello Suite No. 1, is categorized as pure music. Anyone reading this book is likely to recognize that modern culture places an extremely high value on such music. Furthermore, sophisticated music lovers are expected to appreciate pure music and to prefer it to other music. For the sake of simplicity, let's call someone who think this way a "purist."

Purity contrasts with heterogeneity, mixture, contamination, and pollution. Purism makes no sense unless we can say what contaminates music and makes it impure. The answer might seem obvious: it is impure if we add anything that isn't music. For example, suppose I decide to listen to Bach's Cello Suite No. 1, and I play it while viewing the media software program on my computer. The software includes a visualization program. When it plays sounds without associated video, the media program "interprets" the tempo and intensity of the music with a kaleidoscope of colored geometric patterns. In an earlier era, the Disney film *Fantasia* provided frolicking fawns and centaurs to illustrate Ludwig van Beethoven's "Pastoral" symphony, but used abstract geometric figures in motion to accompany Bach's *Toccata and Fugue in D Minor*. As explained by music critic Deems Taylor in a book published to coincide with the film's release, Bach's keyboard music is inherently different from Beethoven's sixth symphony. Beethoven provided a descriptive program linking each symphonic movement to an event, so that the fourth movement is to be understood as a musical presentation of a thunderstorm. In contrast, Bach's *Toccata and Fugue* "bore no title . . . evoked no definite action, told no story." It was, therefore, "abstract music" that called for "abstract representation." Whether we call it "pure" or "abstract" or "absolute," music like Bach's *Toccata and Fugue* is supposed to contrast with music that tells a story or represents a definite action. More generally, music is regarded as impure whenever it represents or symbolizes anything outside itself. In short, music is impure whenever the listening experience has a program—a text providing directions for narrative interpretation—or some other means of conveying definite extra-musical ideas. Except for the few songs that restrict the vocalizing to nonsense syllables and scatting, songs are therefore impure. Opera, too. For similar reasons, ballet and other music-accompanied dance is impure art.

Given this outlook, the rise of purism in nineteenth-century Europe elevated some music at the expense of most music. For purists, Wagner was completely wrong to promote music's supporting role in a *Gesamtkunstwerk*, a mixed-media work. The Wagnerian ideal is merely a composer-sanctioned, high-class version of the fawns and centaurs in the *Fantasia* treatment of Beethoven's "Pastoral." The geometric shapes attached to Bach's music in *Fantasia* are no better. The visualization program bundled into my computer's media software merely automates the process. They all contaminate the purity of the experience by providing extra-musical reference.

Judging by patterns of radio programming and sales figures in the music industry—and, today, we must add patterns of downloading of recorded music—purism is an ideal with few practitioners. Instrumental music is not popular compared with music with lyrics. The most popular instrumental music is movie soundtrack music, which listeners associate with specific stories, characters, and actions. Yet even here, the all-time most popular soundtrack recording, *Titanic*, sold twelve copies for every copy of the most popular instrumental soundtrack, *Star Wars*. Sales of *Titanic* were driven by the presence of a theme song, with lyrics sung by Céline Dion. Turning to classical music, one of the biggest sellers of the past twenty years is the London Sinfonietta's recording of Henryk Górecki's third symphony, a work for orchestra and soprano vocalist. However, its sales are less than half of those of *Star Wars*. Norman Lebrecht estimates that a single pop group, the Beatles, outsold all classical recordings produced in the history of recorded music. These patterns confirm Frank Zappa's cynical advice to would-be composers: "we live in a society where instrumental music is irrelevant—so if a guy expects to earn a living by providing musical entertainment for folks in the USA, he'd better figure out how to do something with a human voice plopped on it." Zappa recognizes that there is limited appreciation of pure music.

At the risk of caricature, the purist looks at these patterns of musical taste and concludes that most people do not appreciate music as music. Most people have the listening skills of the uninformed student who regards the Bach Prelude as nothing but sawing on a big fiddle.

Without being hasty in taking sides for or against purism, its core idea generates an interesting puzzle. And it is not an issue restricted to a subset of classical music. If the musical purity of Mstislav Rostropovich's performance of Bach's Prelude is violated by interpreting it visually, as many Bach lovers feel about Yo-Yo Ma's film *The Music Garden* (2005), then the objection is no less valid about imposing *Fantasia*-style animation on Jaco Pastorius's version of "Donna Lee." However, if a purist objects to visual interpretation, then it seems equally objectionable to provide verbal descriptions of the music. Descriptions and labels can be as "polluting" as pictures. But then how can we endorse listening that is informed by descriptive language, such as "Baroque prelude" and "an electric bass arrangement of a bebop piece for alto saxophone"? Don't they also constitute impure intrusions into the experience of the music? Consider Jacques Barzun's claim that a piece of instrumental music follows a program as soon as the composer thinks of it as an overture, or as a fantasia or fantasy, as in a *Symphonie fantastique*. Even if it is unclear whether the music is "about" something non-musical, its composition is controlled by ideas supplied by language use, and appreciative listening is language-dependent.

In response to these points, purists divide into two camps. Some art lovers defend the extreme view that the pure arts of abstract painting and absolute music are best appreciated with maximum receptivity. For them, pure responses are incompatible with educated responses. Viewing and listening are spoiled by the imposition of technical vocabulary, classifications, and descriptions that interfere with the purity of their perceptual response. However, there is an opposing position that I'll call sophisticated purism. Sophisticated purists do not endorse ignorance. Genuine appreciation of Bach's Prelude responds to it abstractly and not representationally, but appreciation is enhanced by the information that it is Baroque music and that the prelude is a kind of fantasia with a free rhythm (and not, by way of contrast, a rondo-form gavotte with a fixed dance rhythm). It might also be important to think about the fact that it is one of the earliest solo works written for the cello, just as I suggested of Pastorius's version of "Donna Lee" that it is important to understand that it is an electric bass arrangement of a bebop piece for the alto saxophone.

So we face a dilemma. On the one hand, there is a case to be made that a commitment to the importance of pure music is inconsistent with our practice of encouraging the acquisition of a technical vocabulary to talk about it. On the other hand, if classificatory and descriptive language is permissible, where do we draw the line? If the point of the technical talk is to guide perception of the music, why isn't it equally valid to use lyrics and visual cues to guide listening? Whether my visit to the symphony is informed by talk of toccatas and fugues, by a printed musical score, or by a visual story about centaurs, *something* non-musical is guiding my understanding and altering the experience. So we should applaud Yo-Yo Ma's attempt to make Bach more accessible by commissioning films that illustrate the Bach Cello Suites. To be plausible, sophisticated purism must provide reasonable criteria for distinguishing between guidance that facilitates listening and intrusions that detract from it. As a step in that direction, we must explore the issue of how language guides thought and perception.

III. THE INTERSECTION OF LANGUAGE AND THOUGHT

As in Chapter 1, I think it helps to begin with a topic other than music. Consider the students who study at Harvard University. How good are they? Reflecting on his career as a professional philosopher, Robert Paul Wolff challenges the myth that Harvard and other top-ranked colleges are highly selective, with a student body comprised of the best of the best. Wolff observes,

> My own experience is that in the classes I have taught at Harvard, Chicago, Wellesley, and Columbia, there is a huge gap in excellence between the "A" students and the [remainder]. . . . My criticisms of the work of the best deal with nuances of style and subtleties of

argumentation. Those at the other end of the scale are still struggling to master the syntactical structure of English sufficiently to make elementary logical distinctions.

Wolff was not teaching English. He was teaching philosophy. However, in order to succeed in philosophy, students must be sensitive to subtleties of language structure. To consider a simple case, consider the difference that arises by switching the word order of "my mother's cousin's husband" to "my cousin's mother's husband." These two phrases mention the same three relationships, yet they usually refer to completely different people. It is unlikely that anyone could even conceive of this difference in the absence of words to describe them. Wolff is interested in logical relationships and he is making the parallel point that there are logical distinctions and relationships that cannot be understood by someone who is insensitive to linguistic subtleties. In short, some concepts and some cognition are not available in the absence of the possession of language use.

As an example of Wolff's point, consider the following sentences, which are very similar. Yet they make radically different commitments about the upcoming evening.

- I will go to tonight's symphony concert if they are playing Beethoven and Glinka.
- I won't go to the symphony tonight unless they are playing Beethoven or Glinka.

In the first sentence, the presence of both composers in the concert program is sufficient for attending. It leaves it open whether the speaker will be equally willing to go upon learning that the concert program includes some of Frank Zappa's chamber music. The second sentence says that presence of at least one of the two is necessary. However, unlike the first, it does not commit the speaker to going to the concert if Mikhail Glinka's *Spanish Overture No. 1* is being performed. It merely says that the speaker won't attend without music by one of those two composers. Zappa won't be enough.

I want to be very clear about the point of this example. Someone who does not grasp the difference between "unless" and "if" is doomed to confusion concerning the logical difference between necessity and sufficiency when relating one set of circumstances to another. More importantly, neither of these logical relationships can even be *thought* by someone who does not have language in which to express them. (Obviously, I do not mean that a language lacking the specific word "if" is incapable of expressing the sufficiency relationship. Different languages have different expressions for this relationship and some languages, English included, have multiple expressions for it.)

With music, the parallel issue is whether there are any *musical* relationships that become evident only for listeners who employ appropriate vocabulary. To put it another way, does my lack of a descriptive vocabulary ever demonstrate that I do not adequately comprehend the music that I hear? Are there important musical features and relationships that cannot be heard by those who cannot describe them? I think so, and I propose that some of them are surprisingly basic to our engagement with music.

Let's begin with a simple example that supports the necessity of acquiring some descriptive language. Consider the terms "tuning" and "playing." As verbs, they classify actions. But classifying actions involves more than describing what can be directly perceived in a situation. As a college instructor, I watch for hand motions from students that signal a desire to speak. Sometimes when I turn to a student who is waving her hand and call on her to speak, she will decline and will explain that she was merely stretching her arm. In other cases, the same motion is a request to speak. Although the visible behavior is identical, the actions of stretching and signaling are very different actions. Similarly, audiences who arrive at a concert before it begins will sometimes hear the musicians tuning their instruments. This action is not to be confused with playing music. It is an action taken in preparation for playing music, so that none of the musicians will be out of tune. Yet there are times when some members of some audiences cannot tell the difference. There is more to the difference than meets the ears.

For proof that the difference is not self-evident, locate either the audio or film recording of *The Concert for Bangladesh*, a charity concert staged by former-Beatle George Harrison in 1971. Listen to the concert's opening music ensemble, a sitar and sarod duet by Indian musicians Ravi Shankar and Ali Akbar Khan. After Shankar asks the American crowd to listen respectfully, the three stringed instruments produce a short passage of sound. When they stop, much of the crowd applauds. "Thank you," Shankar says. "If you appreciate the tuning so much, I hope you'll enjoy the playing more." The quartet then plays the featured piece of music, "Bangla Dhun," a lengthy improvisation based on a Bengali folk tune. (I return to the topic of high culture poaching folk melodies a bit later in this chapter.)

Was Shankar's joke a prepared response to Western audiences who misapplied the concept of *playing* music to the situation of *tuning* music? Given the laughter it incites in his ensemble, the joke was probably spontaneous. Either way, the joke presupposes that the audience understands the distinction between tuning and playing. Yet the concept of tuning is a complex complement to the idea of playing. To possess a concept of tuning, one must understand the need to tune some instruments together, which requires prior understanding of how ensembles can be in tune and out of tune, together with the idea that some instruments do not hold their tuning. Furthermore, tuning is a preparatory action. In tuning, the sounds are not produced for the audience. In playing, they are. Someone who does not grasp how tuning relates to playing does not know which sounds matter in the relationship between musician and audience. And someone who does not know this is not really hearing music when it is played. There is such a thing as getting it wrong when presented with music, and it is safe to say that not understanding whether the music has even started counts as getting it wrong.

Returning explicitly to the issue about language acquisition, the point is not about the actual word "tuning." Some musicians might tune without using that word. They might "harmonize" or "get it together" or even "get ready." The point is that the language picks out a highly specialized action that exists only in relation to other actions, *and that it is not possible for us to attain this level of conceptual specificity without language.* Tuning and playing are a mere starting point. Most musical cultures make a further distinction between practicing and performing, and so on with many subtle distinctions. With respect to language, then, musical understanding is very much like philosophical understanding.

To borrow from Wittgenstein again, suppose a dog hears a sound at the door. The dog believes that his owner has come home. But, Wittgenstein wonders, "can he also believe his master will come the day after tomorrow?" No, the dog cannot think this thought, because the dog cannot encode a thought with that level of complexity. And the dog cannot formulate that thought because it cannot combine symbols in a language. If Wittgenstein's point is not persuasive, change "the day after tomorrow" to "the second Wednesday of July" and tell me that dogs can form the thought expressed by that phrase. We cannot pinpoint a particular day in the future without the complex clauses that language encodes. The same holds, I have argued, for any informed response to a musical ensemble's activity of tuning. Our musical lives contain many kinds of musical activity, and it is often the case that audible musicality is insufficient to guide the kind of attention demanded by a particular situation. A simple word can rely on complex systems of relationships. As "Wednesday" refers to a location within a seven-day week and "July" refers to a month in a cyclical calendar, "tuning" and "playing" refer to different actions within a culture of music performance.

My emphasis on the words "tuning" and "playing" and their corresponding concepts is unusual. The topic of language's role in music perception is more commonly approached by focusing on terminology for musical structures and relationships. This terminology might seem to be the real issue on the grounds that it describes the music rather than the musicians and their activity, as I have done. However, the same point emerges when we examine musical structure. For example, the concept of the dominant seventh chord of the C major scale is a technical, language-dependent relationship that only arises within a particular musical practice. A chord that combines a dominant triad with the requisite fourth note— the seventh above the root—is employed by musicians in many musical cultures. However, this combination of notes exemplifies the specific relationship described as "the dominant seventh chord of the C major scale" only if the musical culture employs diatonic harmony. Better yet, this chord can be conceptualized as a major/minor seventh chord only if the culture has adopted the modern European system of equal temperament. (By analogy, the act of grabbing someone's arm is only assault and battery in the context of a legal culture that recognizes the appropriate language-dependent concepts.) Lacking the appropriate classificatory concepts that make sense of a system of well-tempered scales, there is no major/minor seventh chord in medieval church music or Hindustani classical music.

My suspicion is that language describing musical activity is more important than technical description of musical structures. For example, if Wagner is correct in the following claim about Beethoven's ninth symphony, then its appreciation requires conceptual specificity, which in turn seems to require quite a lot of technical vocabulary. But, as Stephen Davies wonders, is it really all that technical? Wagner writes,

> If one takes a closer look at the ruling motives in the Allegro itself, one will always find them dominated by a singing quality derived from the Adagio. Beethoven's most significant Allegro movements are mostly governed by a root-melody, belonging in a deeper sense to the character of the Adagio.

How much of this language applies only to music? "Melody" does, in its central meaning, but what of "motives," "Adagio," and "Allegro"? But this last pair is merely foreign, not technical. They are merely the Italian for "slow" and "fast," respectively. If the musical experience requires a language-dependent classification of tempo, then we require extra-musical vocabulary extended to music. Similarly, "motive" is general in its application—so much so that my *Oxford Dictionary of Music* contains no entry for it. Still, I suppose there are those who might need to be clued in that it means a distinctive phrase. Wagner is saying that the important musical phrases in the fast sections of Beethoven's multi-section works are variations of melodies from that work's slow section. Wagner is directing us to listen for an underlying, uniting structure. That is an interesting empirical hypothesis, but it's certainly not an idea that is technical in being music-specific. Wagner is appealing to a general principle of unity of artistic form. I can teach you the relevant concept by examining poetry or by showing you a movie that has two scenes that share parallel editing. It's a point about the way that repetitions of local structures provide unity to complex works of human imagination, and not a technical point about music.

My argument comes down to this. There might be some highly specialized situations in which an appropriate response to music requires technical terminology that picks out features unique to music. However, there is no situation in which this terminology is sufficient, because the specialized terminology does not get a foothold unless we also have terms like "tuning," "practicing," and "playing," which are not unique to music. Socrates had it right when he asked how anyone could believe in flute playing while denying the existence of flute players. In the absence of terms and concepts about music making, the experience of musicality is less than an experience of music.

IV. KNOWING-THAT AND KNOWING-HOW

In this section I will clarify the proposal that appreciation requires more than technical knowledge of the kind exemplified by the concept of the dominant seventh chord of the C major scale. I am arguing that additional language-based concepts are required. However, I am not saying that language acquisition is sufficient. For reasons explained earlier, I think that appreciative listening depends on a pre-existing ability to grasp the musicality of sound. After all, individuals with congenital amusia do not overcome the condition by acquiring new language skills. The opposite is the case: the amusia prevents them from acquiring that language and thus knowing the music.

The issue, then, is the relationship between two modes of knowing: conceptual knowing-that and practical knowing-how. When I know *that* something is the case, I have a fact at my disposal. For example, I know that some runners can go a mile in less than four minutes. I also know that Roger Bannister was the first human to do so in a timed run. However, I do not myself know *how* to accomplish a four-minute mile. In theory, I know how—one simply runs fast. But that is merely a re-description of my initial case of knowing-that: I know that it can be done, and I know how fast one must run in order to accomplish it. However, genuine knowing-how is a matter of being able to do something at will. I cannot run a four-minute mile. In short, knowing-that does not guarantee knowing-how. An individual with congenital amusia might memorize the fact that a melody is a distinctive sequence of pitched sounds, and that Beethoven used variants of the same melody in three different works—in the song "Gegenliebe," in the "Chorale Fantasy" of 1808, and as the "Ode to Joy" theme of the ninth symphony. Yet the amusia prevents the application of the knowledge. It remains merely theoretical if one cannot say, for instance, "Here it is!" at appropriate times when hearing recordings of each work. But if it remains merely theoretical, knowing numerous facts about that melody does not constitute musical understanding of that melody.

To summarize this point in the standard jargon of philosophers, possession of relevant theoretical, propositional knowledge about music is necessary but not sufficient for practical knowledge of how to hear it. Many things are insufficient for achieving a goal, yet required. Having tens of millions of dollars does not guarantee that I can buy a painting by Johannes Vermeer. They are few in number and it is quite possible that none of them will be on the art market. Nonetheless, having tens of millions is certainly required to buy one, should one want one. Analogously, perhaps you never intend to listen to the Prelude from J.S. Bach's Cello Suite No. 1 or the Shankar–Khan performance of "Bangla Dhun." But if you do, you must know that certain things are true of the music if you are to have any chance of knowing how to listen to it.

Furthermore, the Shankar–Khan example illustrates that someone can know how to listen to music without knowing how to listen to all music. I am not talking about the etiquette of concert attendance. Knowing how to listen to Shankar's music requires knowing that the tuning of instruments serves a particular purpose, that sitars and sarods are among them, that their tuning normally takes place on stage as a prelude to the performance, and that the sounds coming from the instruments have different purposes during tuning and playing. Appreciating music requires much more than hearing structural relationships among notes. It requires understanding when sounds are intended for an audience, and when they are not, and attending accordingly.

These judgments about human agency depend on complex judgments about time relationships. Earlier, I introduced Wittgenstein's example of a dog's inability to form expectations about the day after tomorrow. It illustrates that our experience of time is influenced by language. Recognition and evaluation of human agency is another place where concepts about time relationships shape our response. A human form of life is fundamentally connected to our ability to think about complex relationships among past, present, and future events. Our musical lives are no exception.

Once again, the central point is best understood by looking at something other than music. Our emotional lives are shaped by our judgments about what others are doing to us and what we think we are doing to them. Philosophers from Aristotle through the present have emphasized that our emotional states don't simply occur, as changes that just happen to happen. We are not the passive victims of our own feelings of grief or joy. We are the agents of our emotions, because we are the sources of the judgments that inform them. Judgments about the future can be crucial. As Robert Solomon observes, "emotions include intentions for the future." Emotions direct action. For example, anger and embarrassment dispose us toward very different patterns of action. Anger encourages violence, whereas embarrassment encourages concealment. Suppose you catch me eating the leftover cheesecake that you put in the workplace refrigerator. My embarrassment involves more than blushing and feeling a certain way. I am disposed to try to hide my inappropriate behavior. I thrust the cheesecake back into the refrigerator and hurriedly reach for my own lunch. If I think it's too late and I've been caught red-handed, I stammer out an apology. But these responses are irrational unless I believe that your anger might lead you to tell people, thus disrupting my future interactions with people who know that I steal cheesecake.

I'll delay additional discussion of connections between music and emotion until Chapter 3. For now, the point is that emotions reflect our sense of how the past and the present are linked to a possible future. Like Wittgenstein's example of believing that an event will take place on a future date, the embarrassed thief illustrates that a seemingly automatic response can reflect the guidance of language. I can't be embarrassed about stealing your cheesecake unless I know the language of possessive pronouns and the verb "steal" (or some equivalent) as my entry into thinking about property ownership and its violation. Furthermore, you will not be angry about my stealing from you unless your perception is informed by parallel, language-dependent thinking.

To avoid a standard misunderstanding, I will address an objection. It is often argued that emotions are universal human traits, and therefore embarrassment cannot depend on language use. But that objection misses the point, which is that language extends the innate capacity into situations that only exist in a particular, complex world of social interaction. My point is that, similarly, a huge gulf separates an infant's innate capacity to perceive simple rhythms and melodies from the appreciation of improvisational interplay between Ravi Shankar and Ali Akbar Khan during "Bangla Dhun." Even here, "improvisational interplay" describes human agency. The universality of emotion does not determine which episodes of eating cheesecake will produce embarrassment, and the universality of music does not provide us all that we need to appreciate music.

V. FOUR DIMENSIONS OF MUSIC

Here are four very different dimensions of music.

- Local musical properties.
- Large-scale structures.

- Aesthetic properties.
- Historical relationships.

This list is not intended to be exhaustive. It merely distinguishes four kinds of properties that are important in the experience of music. For each category, we can identify cases where language acquisition informs knowing how to hear them in music. In other words, I have selected these four categories because each one illustrates that language acquisition can be a necessary condition for experiencing the music with basic understanding.

Don't get me wrong. I'm not saying every aspect of musical understanding is influenced by language. If that were the case, then informed listeners would never experience musical ineffability. Yet ineffability is common, a point that is explored in Chapter 4. Furthermore, it is obvious that a great deal of musical perception operates independently from language acquisition. After all, most pre-linguistic children can synchronize movements to a rhythm. And let's not forget that mockingbirds can copy the songs of other bird species. They also mimic other distinctive pitch sequences, such as car alarms. So it is clear that perceiving and remembering distinctive sonic patterns is sometimes independent of language use.

This section focuses on language and local musical properties. I will concentrate on the way that music unfolds in time. Local musical properties are local in the sense that, at any given time, we can directly perceive their presence or absence. This category includes melodies and rhythms. To perceive these, we must attend to a sequence of sounds. It must be perceived as both changing (for without change there is no difference that will support differentiation) and patterned (for without pattern the sequence is not distinctive). Yet we cannot take notice of auditory change unless we can have experiences that persist beyond the present instant of time. Rather obviously, a capacity to form short-term memories underlies perception of local musical properties such as a melody or a rhythm. We must store relevant experiences in our memory long enough to compare that memory with what comes next.

For example, perception of musical rhythm requires awareness of re-occurring stresses within a pattern of sound. It therefore requires awareness of more than whatever is simultaneously before us at just one moment. To hear a rhythm one must experience a change, remember it, recognize that it is repeated, and then anticipate its continuation. (Psychologists debate the precise length of the fraction of a second that is experienced as an immediate moment in which change is perceived, but the answer to that question should not impact the philosophical point I'm advancing.) To borrow a point from Jerrold Levinson, the experience of music requires a capacity for *quasi-hearing*, which is the capacity "of seeming to hear a span of music" by knowing how to attend to a connected series of moment-to-moment changes. Quasi-hearing is the capacity of knowing how to "aurally synthesize . . . music surrounding any present instant" within the musical sequence.

Quasi-hearing is important because it generates the experience of a connected flow of coherent sound. Without quasi-hearing, we would hear moment-to-moment sonic changes but we would never hear melodies. We would not hear beginnings, endings, and transitions. For example, one of the most memorable moments in Mikhail Glinka's *Spanish Overture No. 1* is the entrance of castanets in triple time around the three-minute mark. Someone with amusia can hear a change at this point—after all, an additional, distinctive noise enters the mix of sound. Someone who hears music hears something more. She hears a pause that signals a transitional moment, followed by a tempo increase and the entrance of rapid percussion with a distinctive rhythm. Since the same sound waves reach both listeners, the experiential difference depends on what the second listener knows how to do, which is how to group the sounds and to anticipate further sounds as a result.

However, it appears that listening requires the guidance of descriptive language as soon as the music takes on any degree of complexity, employing structures and relationships that take us beyond very simple cases of quasi-hearing. To borrow from Stephen Davies, most music that's worth hearing calls upon our ability to discriminate among musical properties with "a higher order of complexity: themes, developments, modulations, harmonic resolutions, and so on." For example, there is a huge difference between being aware that music is returning to a familiar melody and being aware that the music has arrived at the recapitulation in a first-movement sonata form. The latter awareness involves expectations and understanding that the former lacks. Yet it seems to me that someone who is literally unable to articulate the concept of the arrival of the recapitulation has about as much chance of forming the mental expectations appropriate to that event as my dog has of forming the thought that I will return home from my next conference trip on the second Sunday of the month. Again, it is not a matter of specific words and phrases. Someone who does not know the phrase "the arrival of the recapitulation" might have a different, equally appropriate description.

This last point extends to awareness of many local musical properties. If a melodic gestalt is a local property, then so are many of the standard means of providing a development of it. Many heavy metal guitarists have sufficient training to talk about their reliance on inversions and retrograde variations in their music solos. Granted, few metal fans know those words. However, Davies notes, the level of discrimination required to perceive thematic retrograde and inversion requires *some* ability to label the difference. Davies does not use the example of heavy metal, but even here we have an audience full of people who hear the difference between a coherent guitar solo and a random spewing of notes. An appreciative fan might talk about places where the tune goes backwards and then upside down, or employ some other equally apt description. However, without *some* words to describe it, the fans are not going to possess the foundational concept of a sequence that retains its internal relationship despite radical perceptual change. Without this sort of practiced, linguistically guided understanding, listening to most instrumental music must involve extraordinarily superficial perception. Such listening might permit someone to recognize that the "Ode to Joy" theme isn't the same as "The Star Spangled Banner," but there will be little or no awareness of the specifics that make them different. The listener's experience will be as uninformed and unjustified as that of concert-goers who applaud the tuning of a sitar.

VI. HISTORY, STYLE, AND AESTHETIC PROPERTIES

Listening becomes more complex when we consider historical and aesthetic properties and their interconnections.

Historical properties are essentially bound up with the time and place of an object's origination. Authorship is a prime example. It is an important historical property of musical works. Earlier, I mentioned Bach's *Toccata and Fugue in D Minor*. Some scholars suspect that Bach was not the composer. Among other clues, the structure and harmonies are much too simple. Or, if by Bach, it was a violin piece that someone else transcribed for organ. Cases like these remind us that an artwork's historical properties are not immediately apparent. In contrast, aesthetic properties are elements of the experience and so they directly affect the quality of an experience. Beauty and ugliness are central examples. There is also the stately quality of the *Toccata and Fugue*, the gracefulness of so much of W.A. Mozart's music, or the concision of the Ramones' song "Teenage Lobotomy." Because the stateliness and concision are perceivable, one might conclude that aesthetic properties differ from historical ones in being experientially self-evident. However, as with historical properties, it's possible to overlook or misperceive aesthetic properties.

Kendall Walton offers the example of piano music. Some piano music is aesthetically delicate. Examples include the piano compositions of Claude Debussy that he described as "hammerless." There is also the early piano music of Erik Satie. However, pianos are tuned percussion instruments. They produce sound because pressure on the keys drives hammers against taught strings. To someone with congenital amusia, there is nothing delicate about any piano music. It all sounds pretty much the way it sounds to me when the cat walks across the keyboard. Nonetheless, Satie's three *Gymnopédies* are frequently described as delicate. The delicacy of piano music is relative to the medium. This delicacy is an aesthetic property that is apparent only through comparative listening, through contrast with other piano music. Although the playing of

New Orleans legend James Booker is a marvel, it has never been described as delicate. (I recommend lending an ear to Booker's romp though Chopin's "Minute Waltz.") Again, the point is not whether one uses the actual term "delicate." It is that language use is a prerequisite for the conceptual fine-tuning that underlies the appropriate, complex comparative judgments that inform the aesthetic experience of delicate piano music.

Returning to my claim that historical authorship has aesthetic relevance, consider these facts. Some of Dmitri Shostakovich's music contains the progression D, E flat, C, B natural. In German musical notation, the sequence is D, Es, C, H, which can be read as "D. Sch." Because Shostakovich was a Soviet composer, the motif is recognized as one of many means by which he inserted slyly subversive elements into music that was expected to communicate social harmony and progress to the culturally illiterate masses. Appearances of the motif in Shostakovich's tenth symphony and first cello concerto invite knowledgeable listeners to interpret these passages as denoting the composer and as evidence that he is saying something about his own life. The motif gives his music an aesthetic expressiveness it would otherwise lack. Thus, historical location shapes meanings, which in turn generate aesthetic properties, such as expressive properties that would otherwise not arise.

Generalizing, many aesthetic properties are only perceived by listeners who know about a musical work's history. Getting an aesthetic property right is frequently a matter of being aware of the music's real history. It can be a matter of knowing who wrote it, and when, and which musical resources were available in that time and place. This information often conflicts with relationships suggested by the sound of the music. Peter Van der Merwe cites the old joke—which he remarks is "not entirely a joke"—that most Spanish music is composed beyond the borders of Spain. Musical styles do not stay put in their place of origin.

With this in mind, consider a case in which musical originality or novelty is one of a work's aesthetic virtues. All music is derivative in some way from other music, and thus any music's degree of originality is as much a matter of aesthetic as of historical judgment. However, ignorance about history can create a false impression of novelty or its close cousins, incoherence and weirdness. Here, aesthetic properties are shaped by historical ones. How much novelty is there in Glinka's *Spanish Overture No. 1*? If you've never heard Spanish music, the entrance of castanets must seem extremely novel. Similarly, ignorance of the melodic origins of the music's main theme will make it seem novel, too. However, it is the *jota aragonesa*, a Spanish tune that Glinka transposed from guitar strings to plucked orchestral strings. These elements of Glinka's composition are appropriations that place it in the category of the exotic. Granted, there is an element of novelty in his decision to orchestrate Spanish folk music and thus bring it into the mainstream of Western music. In this respect, there is far less originality in Alexis-Emmanuel Chabrier's *España* of 1883, for it exhibits the influence of Glinka's overture of 1845. To turn it around and to hear it as Glinka borrowing from Chabrier would result in an underestimation of Glinka's degree of originality. Chabrier may have heard peasants playing the *jota aragonesa* during his 1882 visit to Spain, but one does not hear *España* correctly if one praises Chabrier's originality in transplanting the folk tune and rhythm into an orchestral work. The error would be something like watching the film *O Brother, Where Art Thou?* because you're a George Clooney fan, and then praising Ethan and Joel Coen for their originality in making a film about an escape from a Mississippi chain gang. Better-informed viewers understand that the film reflects a tradition of earlier movies, most notably I Am a Fugitive from a Chain Gang (1932) and Preston Sturges's film Sullivan's Travels (1941). While a superficial viewing of O Brother is not worthless, it will be a very partial response to the aesthetic complexity that actually emerges from the cultural interplay of several historically embedded artworks.

Awareness of a complex chain of causality—Spanish folk music to Chabrier by way of Glinka—is literally unthinkable in the absence of appropriate linguistic resources. For example, in English we convey the proper relationships with prepositions. Furthermore, one ought to possess the concepts of folk music and of musical orchestration, and have some sense of the cultural divide at play in that distinction. A listener's ignorance of influence will result in aesthetic error. Thus Van der Merwe makes the point that William Byrd's "The Bagpipe and the Drone" from The Battle sounds like Spanish music, but isn't. It is simply old enough to employ musical cadences that subsequently fell out of favor everywhere except Spain.

Here is a different example of how an aesthetic property can emerge from historical origins. Glinka's Spanish Overture No. 1 merges two regional styles. Its sonata form stems from his formal training in "classical" style as regularized by composers of Joseph Haydn's generation. The tunes, the jota rhythm, and the percussion of castanets are adopted from music that Glinka heard in Spain in 1845. Although many classical music lovers will see nothing special about this poaching from "folk" culture, there was no cultural inevitability at work here. The overture inspired a long tradition of "Spanish" caprices. If

Glinka had not gone to Spain, many works by later composers might not exist. To consider a parallel example from popular music, one of Johnny Cash's biggest hits was "Ring of Fire." As recorded by Cash, the song's structure, rhythm, and core instrumentation are standard country and western. But the opening moments of Cash's 1963 recording are stylistically surprising. It begins with a trumpet fanfare in the style of Mexican mariachi music. A short fanfare reappears three times. Expanded, it replaces Cash's voice when he should deliver the second verse. So the arrangement is a bizarre juxtaposition of the music of Memphis and Guadalajara. Within its historical context, this merger of styles is as daring as Glinka's overture. However, it can be very difficult to experience their novelty. What is novel in its originating context is hard to hear with fresh "ears" a decade, generation, or century later. Either way, fresh or dated, a musical innovation is only experienced as original and inventive against a background of conceptually informed expectations.

Although such examples are all around us, there is resistance to the idea that background knowledge is needed to appreciate the aesthetic delicacy of Satie's three *Gymnopédies*. However, if such knowledge is irrelevant, then it must also be wrong to admire a musical performer's virtuosity. Without reference to causality, there is no aesthetic relevance to the difference between a sequence of sounds that is difficult to perform and a sequence that sounds *as if* it is difficult to execute. Listen to the fluid, rapid harpsichord solo that begins a minute and a half into the Beatles' "In My Life." But it isn't any such thing. It's an electronic manipulation of music performed at half speed and an octave lower on a Steinway piano. "In My Life" displays musical virtuosity, but not keyboard virtuosity. I defy anyone to form the thoughts required to grasp and appreciate the *studio* virtuosity displayed in "In My Life" and the rest of *Rubber Soul* if the aesthetic response is restricted to the concepts available to a pre-verbal toddler.

VII. MUSIC IS ART, REVISITED

Purists, I have observed, are of two sorts. First, some purists endorse Bell's thesis that pure appreciation requires ignorance or, somehow, a withholding of all acquired concepts. Second, some purists endorse the necessity of acquiring music-specific language and concepts as a condition for listening to pure music with basic understanding. This second, more sophisticated purism requires a distinction between musical and non-musical concepts and terminology. Some music is pure music and can be understood—indeed, is properly understood—without attaching descriptions or concepts that give it extra-musical significance. We might point to Beethoven's variation number 32 in Opus 120, a set entitled *33 Variations on a waltz by Anton Diabelli*. Because listeners ought to think about it and to respond to it as a fugal treatment of a theme that another composer supplied, an appropriate response to these two and a half minutes of music demands a relatively complex cluster of concepts. Although the sophisticated purist challenges the hardcore purist by observing that a basic understanding of the variation number 32 requires guidance from language, music remains pure because it is not about anything except other music. There is no program and nothing like the animation that *Fantasia* imposes on Bach's *Toccata and Fugue in D Minor*.

However, absolute music is a highly specialized category. Above all, we should resist thinking of it as the default category that is present until a composer adds extra-musical content to music. As I noted earlier, the vast majority of people don't care much for "pure" music. That's not surprising. Most people don't care for abstract visual art, either. To appreciate it, we must learn to suspend cognitive processes and expectations that enrich our experiences of most art. But to do that, the response has to be guided by knowledge that some artists expect the audience to respond in this specialized (some would say impoverished) way. Eric Siblin describes the Prelude of Bach's Cello Suite No. 1 as exhibiting "courtly purpose . . . blasted through with rapture." Did Bach want us to think this way about his music? Or are we engaging in Romantic anachronism? The rub is that we cannot decide unless we make a judgment about Bach's intentions. But to ask this question is to leave the realm of musical sound and to talk about the gestures of the people behind it. I cannot tell whether the music makes an extra-musical reference unless I think about human agency.

Here is another formulation of this point. Some pages back, I mentioned that Beethoven used variants of the same melody in three different works—in the song "Gegenliebe," in the "Chorale Fantasy" of 1808, and as the "Ode to Joy" theme of the ninth symphony. However, these aren't variations in the way that Opus 120 contains variations, for they are not intended to be heard *as* variations. But this claim relies upon my judgment about what Beethoven was doing, something that cannot be settled if we withhold extra-musical knowledge. Now consider the fourth movement of the first symphony of Johannes Brahms (Opus 68) and its incorporation of music that sounds like a fourth variation on the same theme. Is this music an astounding coincidence? Or is it plagiarism? Is it a variation, in the way that Diabelli variations are variations but the use of the theme in the "Chorale Fantasy" of 1808 is not?

This is not a trivial matter. It affects the degree of originality present in Brahms's first symphony. In order to decide that it is a variation—and no one thinks otherwise, which is why Brahms said "Every jackass hears that!" when a listener mentioned the similarity to Brahms—we must interpret it as an intentional acknowledgement of Beethoven, the historical individual. In referring to Beethoven, the music makes an extra-musical reference. Therefore a minimally adequate understanding of this symphonic, pure music is guided by concepts that are not unique to musical practice. If the presence of this reference disqualifies this symphony from the category of pure music, the category is rapidly emptying out.

What is ultimately at stake here, Graham McFee notes, is the question of whether pure music should be judged and appreciated as art. Where there is utter musical purity, there is no need to decide which concepts are culturally appropriate to it. That seems to leave us with music that can be understood by pre-linguistic children and some non-human animals. However, it excludes most of the experience of music that gives it significance for most listeners. Because we need to acquire language and cultural understanding in order to operate with the conceptual framework that culturally situates it, such as the difference between practicing music and performing music, then humans and non-human animals employ different cognitive processes in producing and interpreting musical sounds. Music, as we understand it, exists only in the human realm. We have a difference in kind, rather than a difference in degree of musicality. As such, attributing music to birds and whales is an informative anthropomorphism, as a way of thinking about important continuities with other animal species. Kathleen Higgins is particularly insightful about the benefits of admitting that we are not the only species to make music; it can bring home the realization that we "share the world" with them. So the issue of whether mockingbirds and pre-linguistic children perceive music is not a trivial question. They certainly hear some of what is musical in music. But that is not quite the same thing. Mockingbirds can mimic the songs of other birds, proving that they perceive sound structures—and in some sense understand them—in the absence of understanding those structures by virtue of acquiring a technical vocabulary. However, I wager that mockingbirds cannot hear that Satie's piano music is more delicate than Booker's version of the minute waltz.

Three

From my great pain
I make small songs;
They lift their ringing feathers
And flutter to her heart.
                    (Heinrich Heine)

When German poet Heinrich Heine personifies his artistic creations as birds, he introduces a metaphor. But what about his claim that his emotional distress is the material of his songs? Is this to be taken literally, as a theory of artistic inspiration? Or is it another metaphor?

   Although I have thrown cold water on the idea that birds and German poets are kin in their ability to make music, I face a long history of opposition. Some of that opposition arises from the longstanding view that music expresses emotion, and this expressive capacity is the essence of musical art. Many bird lovers endorse it, as well. They believe that birds sing for some reason besides communicating location, staking out territory, and attracting a mate. Like people, birds sing in order to express emotion. In "Ode to a Nightingale," John Keats contends that the bird's music expresses ecstasy. More recently, philosopher David Rothenberg argues that the variations that birds introduce into their songs demonstrate that they are doing more than communicating. Sometimes, it seems as if "birds burst into song out of pure joy," and there is no scientific way to prove otherwise. But why take it as an expression of joy? Because, Rothenberg argues, "Evolution is not supposed to produce beauty for the sake of loveliness alone." In sum, if a nightingale's song is beautiful, and its actual design exceeds what is required by evolutionary adaptation, then it must be an expression of joy, for it must also be doing what people do when they make music.

There is nothing special about Rothenberg's version of the argument that beautiful bird song is a species of expressive art. Many people endorse it. From the perspective of influence, the most important version might be that of Jacques Delamain, the French ornithologist who trained composer Olivier Messiaen to recognize a variety of birdsongs. In the book *Why Birds Sing*, Delamain writes,

> In the rhythmic chime of his clear, rapid, unexpected notes, the Song Thrush encloses all the joy of living, his gay, capricious vehemence; . . . here is the emotional life of the bird at its height: well-being, joy of existence, happiness at feeling in his place in a chosen corner of nature[.] . . . The song, liberating discharge of a vital plenitude that the bird cannot contain, is rendered by the male with attitudes which are often strange, now frenzied, now fixed[.]

Delamain advances three distinct claims in this passage. First, the bird's song displays or reveals its emotional life. Second, the songs display distinct, recognizable emotions that parallel human emotions. In this case, the song displays the bird's joy. Third, the bird cannot contain or control itself. This, Delamain maintains, is how "musical art is born."

This chapter argues that, on the contrary, the natural expressiveness of sound does not support the position that the expression of emotion is the essence of music. If the art of music is born anywhere, it emerges from a society's conventions for adapting music's expressive qualities to its specific purposes. Art reflects culture. Unchecked natural outpourings of emotion are not art.

I. SYMPTOMS AND SYMBOLS

Understanding the debate about musical expression requires a detour into the general topic of expression. Emotions permit expression because emotions embody beliefs and attitudes about events.

Consider a particular sound, made on two different occasions. On Saturday evening, at a chamber music recital, a quartet is about to launch into Henryk Górecki's third string quartet. The first movement begins very softly. Fifteen seconds into it, Frida coughs loudly. People who are seated nearby turn and glare at her. The woman seated beside Frida hands her a cough drop. Two days later, at Monday morning's staff meeting, Frida and her colleagues are discussing impending changes in their office. One of Frida's co-workers begins to say, "We'll have to hire someone for . . .," only to be interrupted when Frida coughs loudly. Frida realizes that her co-worker is about to blurt out a possible plan to re-assign some work duties. Frida thinks that it is not yet time to share those plans. Frida's co-workers get the message and no one pursues the subject of hiring. No one hands Frida a cough drop.

This example illustrates two things. First, there is a difference between someone who is coughing and someone who is imitating or representing themselves as coughing. When Frida coughs on Saturday, the cough is a symptom of discomfort in her throat. The sound that she makes is caused by the discomfort. If she could contain herself, she would not cough, because she knows that it will disturb the audience for the music. She, and everyone else, wants to hear the music. On Monday, she can contain herself. There is no discomfort in her throat. Instead, she does not want her co-worker to continue talking. Her cough is staged to disrupt a line of conversation. The co-worker's understanding of the message depends on understanding that it is not a symptom of a sore throat.

Like many philosophers today, I think that expression requires a mental state with an intentional object. That is, the mental state is directed at something, which is the object of that mental state. I endorse Jesse Prinz's formulation, "The objects of our emotions are the real or imagined conditions that elicit them." Emotions fall into the class of things that can be expressed, then, because they are within the realm of psychological states that judge or evaluate something. An *expressive behavior* is about something because it reflects a mental state that is about something. If we ask what mental state is expressed by Frida's fake cough, we will probably agree that it expresses her annoyance at, and disapproval of, the co-worker's contribution to the conversation. So the staged cough expresses emotion. In contrast, Frida's cough at the concert is not directed at anyone or anything. Consequently, it is a mistake to think that it *expresses* the feeling of dryness or irritation in her throat.

Like a cough or sneeze, many emotions are intimately related to the body. As Peter Goldie summarizes the crucial point, "Many emotions, especially short-term emotions such as fear, anger, and disgust, involve characteristic involuntary bodily changes—muscular reactions, hormonal changes . . . and so on." These involuntary changes are the basis for an emotion's feeling-component. Anger increases the flow of the hormones adrenaline and noradrenaline, causing an angry person to experience an increased heart rate, contributing one element to the cluster that characterizes *feeling* angry. Furthermore, there may be changes that other people can observe, permitting others to detect the emotion. As you become angry, an observer may see bulging neck muscles, flushed red cheeks, and a clenched fist. However, emotions are more than bodily changes that are felt and observed. Although many people use "emotion" and "feeling" as synonymous terms, what follows depends on using the criterion of intentionality or "aboutness" to make a distinction between them. Emotions include feelings, but not every feeling has an intentional object.

In Chapter 2, I explained how emotion involves a belief about how one's past and present are linked to a possible future. For example, when Frida coughs at the concert, the anger of other audience members reflects a judgment that Frida is spoiling things. Given this requirement, there is an important difference between *having the feeling* that is characteristic of anger and actually *being* angry. Given this requirement, the mere presence of a characteristic feeling does not qualify as an emotion. Furthermore, emotions are frequently distinguished from moods, which are longer-term feelings that lack the directed "aboutness" of emotions. Feeling sad following a significant loss is very different from feeling depressed for no particular reason. For purposes of my argument, it is not important whether this distinction is genuine, or whether Jesse Prinz is correct that both emotions and moods have intentional content. However, moods illustrate that there are many complications that arise when we move beyond the most basic emotions, which are my focus here.

Psychologists and philosophers who study emotion generally agree that there are seven simple, core emotions. They are fear, anger, happiness, contempt, surprise, disgust, and sadness. Because they involve involuntary bodily changes, all seven have natural and therefore universal symptoms. The most notable symptoms are our distinctive facial expressions. These are not universal symptoms in the sense that they always occur and are always recognized. Rather, they are universal in the sense that people who can recognize them are equally adept at identifying them cross-culturally. Furthermore, they are natural symptoms, for individuals who are born without sight display the same core repertoire of facial expression as everyone else despite their inability to learn them by watching others. Like everyone else, babies born without sight express happiness with a smiling mouth and a downward shift of the outer corners of the eyebrows, and they express disgust with a wrinkled nose and raised upper lip. These natural facial expressions are our most straightforward, unproblematic examples of human expression of emotion. As a consequence, we are not always the best judges of our own emotions. People have subjective, "internal," first-person access to their own emotions by way of their characteristic feelings. However, the accompanying belief element is often fleeting and it does not always rise to consciousness. So if I am not clear about the judgment I am making, I may be unclear about which emotion is present. Suppose a friend tells me that a mutual acquaintance has been promoted at work. I feel surprised. My friend, watching my face, sees an expression of disgust. In this case, my friend may know better than I do how I feel about the news.

Although facial expression is the paradigm case of expression, it is not always trustworthy. Expression of emotion is culturally influenced—some even say culturally "scripted." Each society develops a set of expectations about proper and improper emotional expressions, including rules concerning how, when, to whom, and to what degree various expressions are permitted. Facial expression is heavily policed by cultural display rules. In many Asian societies, "natural" emotional expression is highly restrained. With many Japanese adults, a strong emotional response is only detectable by watching for fleeting changes around the eyes, if it is to be seen at all. In contrast, Americans feel far freer than almost everyone else to indiscriminately display the core emotions through facial expression.

So far, I have concentrated on basic emotions, which are short-lived responses to immediate circumstances. We also have cognitively complex emotions, such as shame and jealousy. Cognitively complex emotions can involve judgment about complex social relationships that are themselves "scripted" by social rules governing behavior. Cultural context heavily informs both the emotion's arousal and its outward expression. Suppose that Fred, one of Frida's co-workers, starts to make belittling jokes about her job performance after she receives the promotion that he sought. If the jokes are only directed at Frida and only after her promotion, then they are not expressions of his otherwise humorous, teasing nature. They express Fred's jealousy. Yet notice the enormously complex set of concepts that Fred must bring to bear on their respective social standings in order to feel jealous, and the additional complex understanding of workplace politics that directs its outward expression into belittling jokes.

Cultural scripting often converts short-lived emotions into extended episodes of expression. And of course expression becomes even more complicated as different expressive scripts are linked to class and gender. In Victorian England, for example, a respectable widow wore black mourning dress for at least a full year. This full mourning was followed by a year of second mourning, followed by a period of half-mourning. During these two periods, the amount of black fabric was reduced in turn. As an additional expression of her grief, a widow could not remarry for at least two years. In contrast, a widower could express his grief by wearing black gloves and perhaps a black armband for a few months. If he chose to remarry within two years of his wife's death, his new bride was expected to adopt mourning garb for her predecessor. These Victorian rules for the expression of grief can seem overly elaborate, arbitrary, and generally insincere to us now, in the twenty-first century. However, it would be a great error to conclude that they do not count as genuine expressions of grief. Most expressions of emotion are more like Victorian mourning clothes than smiles on faces. If Fred's jokes can express jealousy, then Queen Victoria's decision to wear black for forty years following Prince Albert's death can serve as a sincere expression of her grief.

Three closely related consequences follow from the cultural scripting of expression. Since music is also shot through with cultural scripting, these three points should inform our thinking about music's capacity to express emotion. First, an expression of emotion does not have to express an occurrent feeling. Once we acquire a non-natural method for expressing emotion, the expressive gesture can be detached from the immediate circumstances and emotion, allowing individuals to "express" emotions that they do not possess. The full mourning "weeds" of a Victorian widow continue to express her grief during moments when something makes her happy.

Second, once detachability is in place, the expression can be insincere. Who hasn't said "Thank you" after receiving a gift that one is not thankful for? Third, there will be occasions when what looks to be an expression will not be expression at all. On any given occasion, a behavior or "expression" that is a characteristic symptom or conventional expression of an inner psychological state might be something else altogether. The symptom or convention might be present in the absence of any intention to communicate an emotional state. Lacking that intention, it does not even count as expression at all, not even as an insincere one. (To judge that a smile or another facial expression is insincere, one must believe that the person is intentionally misleading others, and that it is wrong to do so in the relevant circumstances.) The next section explores the idea that music is also a heavily "scripted" expression of emotion, and therefore music that seems to express emotion might not be expressing anything at all.

II. EXPRESSION AND EXPRESSIVE QUALITIES

Let us, at long last, return to music. Consider the Scottish fiddle tune, "The Soldier's Joy." It is appropriately named, for it is expressively joyful. Although several sets of lyrics have been added to it over the years, neither the title nor the lyrics have any bearing on my description of it as joyful music. Given a forced choice from the standard list of core emotions (fear, anger, happiness, contempt, surprise, disgust, and sadness), anyone who hears "The Soldier's Joy" and who does not pick happiness is simply not competent with respect to the basics of Western music. Furthermore, it is *very* happy music, hence joyful.

But how can that be? It cannot experience joy, for it is a rhythmic and melodic pattern. It is no more capable of *being* joyful—of having the emotion of joy—than is a heap of pebbles or the equation "$2 \times 2 = 4$." Nor can it *express* joy, for nothing can express joy unless it satisfies two conditions: it can experience the emotion of joy and it can provide an outward symptom or conventional symbol of that inner state. Since music is not a sentient thing with "inner," psychological states, music cannot satisfy the first of these two conditions for expression. Therefore "The Soldier's Joy" does not express emotion. There is only one way to avoid the conclusion that we talk nonsense whenever we say that the music is joyful or we say that it expresses joy. Our alternative is to deny that we mean what we seem to mean. It will surprise no one when I report that music lovers and philosophers prefer to save the day in this way, by interpreting "The music is joyful" non-literally.

The favored reinterpretation focuses on the meaning of "is" in "'The Soldier's Joy' is joyful." That word can be reinterpreted as short-hand for "is an expression of," so that "'The Soldier's Joy' is joyful" really means "'The Soldier's Joy' is some person's expression of joy." It is just like seeing a festively decorated house in the weeks leading to Christmas and saying, "That house has the Christmas spirit." What we really mean is that whoever decorated the house has the Christmas spirit, and the decorations express that emotional connection to the holiday. (Again, one lesson from the previous section is that the expression might be insincere. The decorations might be the work of someone who despises Christmas but who hopes to win the cash prize given annually to the most festively decorated home. However, the possibility of insincerity arises precisely *because* we treat it as the expression of a particular person's emotion. Insincerity is a species of expression.) Notice, on this account, that an attribution of emotion to music necessarily requires attributing the emotion to the historical individual(s) responsible for the design. So " 'The Soldier's Joy' is joyful" really means " 'The Soldier's Joy' is its composer's expression of joy." On this account, "The Soldier's Joy" is emotionally expressive in roughly the same way that Delamain says that the thrush's song is emotionally expressive.

Many complications disrupt this appealingly simple theory. The important objections arise from the fact that the musical pattern does all the work of communicating the emotion. One might suppose that certain sound patterns are naturally expressive, as the natural, universal analogue to the natural behavior of moving one's mouth into a smile to express happiness. However, just as the mouth can do more than smile and frown, expressive musical patterns have other functions besides expressing emotion. Except in the very limited case of a child's spontaneous facial expression that betrays occurrent emotion, what appears to be an expression of emotion is frequently something other than an expression of emotion. What follows is an explanation of Alan Tormey's important observation, made four decades ago, that the presence of expressive qualities is never sufficient for expression.

My argument depends on separating two features of "The Soldier's Joy" that fulfill two different social functions. First, it is a reel, and I assume that whoever composed it intended it as such, which is to say that it was composed with the intention of functioning to support a specific kind of dancing. As I argued in Chapter 2, that intention reflects a great many concepts about music and its uses. Since this particular reel seems to date back to the middle of the eighteenth century, we can assume that the composer knew the difference between a jig and a reel, two dances with very different time signatures.

Let's assume, therefore, that the composer intended to compose a reel and succeeded (admirably!). The music's second feature is its expressive quality. If you are going to maintain that "'The Soldier's Joy' is joyful" means that it expresses joy, then I assume you are maintaining that the composer intended to express his own personal happiness by creating and sharing this particular piece of music. My alternative proposal is that the composer's success in achieving his rhythmic goal generates the conditions that create the impression that the composer must also have been expressing happiness. Therefore the music's expressive quality of happiness may have been quite unintentional, and therefore the music does not necessarily express happiness.

Because I am contrasting expressive and non-expressive functions, I should say a little more about the functional value of expressing emotion. In particular, consider the point that the functional value of *expressing* emotion is not identical with the value of *experiencing* emotion. The capacity to experience emotion is functionally useful to the individual who has the emotion. Emotion guides behavior by alerting us to the significance of changing situations and by motivating actions in response. We can imagine sentient creatures who have emotions but who do not show them expressively in their bodies. (In societies that suppress the open expression of emotion, this might be regarded as a biological advantage!) So what advantage is gained by our natural proclivity to exhibit emotions? The obvious advantage is that we are social creatures. Consequently, it is useful to be able to "read" the expressions of emotion of people we encounter. That is why children with Asperger's syndrome—characterized by a failure to notice and recognize facial changes that express emotion— are laboriously taught what other children learn spontaneously.

However, looking at faces and body language is a very limited mode of access. It limits us to knowledge about occurrent emotions of people near us. So there is a social benefit to designing public signals that communicate emotions. Music is one of the media we employ for this purpose. Steven Feld has documented the social use of a particular falling melodic phrase by the Kaluli people of Papua New Guinea.

In a ritualized use of music, a Kaluli woman who is distressed by a death or another significant loss begins to weep. Then she begins to sing the distinctive descending phrase, transforming her weeping into singing. This musical phrase is adapted from the song of the fruitdove, which Kaluli interpret as genuine expressions of grief by birds, some of whom possess the souls of dead humans. Next, the woman improvises a song. This sung-weeping and singing sets off a prolonged event that ignores the performer–audience boundaries typical in modern musical culture. Other women respond with weeping and melodic wailing. Men, who are normally the musicians of Kaluli society, do not respond with melody. Instead, they weep hysterically, without singing. Feld explores multiple social benefits to this use of music, including the way it reverses normal Kaluli social patterns by demanding public confirmation of women's emotions.

The functional value of conventionalized expression requires members of a society to agree on its expressive character. In contemporary life, for example, music is routinely attached to mass communication. A political candidate might use "The Soldier's Joy" as background music in a television advertisement with a positive message about better times to come. The same tune will never be used as the background music for an "attack" advertisement that presents an opponent in a negative light, for that would send a mixed message that would confuse potential voters. Yet in order for music to be expressively useful in mass media, something in the general pattern of the music has to communicate its expressive character. It cannot always depend on some prior social conditioning that associates a particular melody with a particular expressive function—the way, for example, that the red octagon of the stop sign is a purely conventional symbol for stopping. If it is to be useful in an advertisement, "The Soldier's Joy" has to be univocally expressive for millions of people who do not otherwise listen to bluegrass and Scottish folk music. Similarly, there would be little point to hiring composers to write original film scores if music does not possess distinctive expressive qualities that supplement and enhance the visual and narrative material. Suppose the ominous quality of the "Imperial March"—Darth Vader's theme in the *Star Wars* films—is established through association, because it accompanies Vader's appearance. If that is why the music is ominous, then there's no point in hiring John Williams to write the music and then hiring an orchestra to play the theme, for the film audience will already have to know how they feel about Vader before the music functions expressively. The same point applies to songwriting. The melody that Woody Guthrie supplied to "Dear Mrs. Roosevelt" does not express his sadness about President Roosevelt's death simply because the words express grief; if Guthrie had somehow shoe-horned a lyric about Roosevelt's death into the music of "This Land Is Your Land," the song would simply create cognitive dissonance due to conflicting emotional expression in the words and the melody.

Examples like these show that music has features that make it useful for presenting expressive qualities and that people are generally very good at recognizing these musical features and the resulting expressive character. Previously, I argued that the production and reception of music is shaped by cultural tradition. If we combine these three points, they undercut the idea that "The music is joyful" *always* attributes an expressive function to the music in the strict sense of providing an externalization of a mental state. They demonstrate that an expressive quality of joy may be nothing but a byproduct of a culturally entrenched musical pattern, created for reasons other than expressing emotion. The musical features that prompt us to say that "The Soldier's Joy" is joyful might be present for reasons that have absolutely nothing to do with the expression of joy.

"The Soldier's Joy" was already at least a century old when Thomas Hardy described a performance of it in the novel *Far from the Madding Crowd*, written in 1874.

> Here sat three fiddlers, and beside them stood a frantic man with his hair on end, perspiration streaming down his cheeks, and a tambourine quivering in his hand. The dance ended, and on the black oak floor in the midst a new row of couples formed for another.
>
> "Now, ma'am, and no offence I hope, I ask what dance you would like next?" said the first violin.
>
> "Really, it makes no difference," said the clear voice of Bathsheba . . .
>
> "Then," said the fiddler, "I'll venture to name that the right and proper thing is 'The Soldier's Joy'—there being a gallant soldier married into the farm—hey, my sonnies, and gentlemen all?" . . .
>
> So the dance began. As to the merits of "The Soldier's Joy," there cannot be, and never were, two opinions. It has been observed in the musical circles of Weatherbury

and its vicinity that this melody, at the end of three-quarters of an hour of thunderous footing, still possesses more stimulative properties for the heel and toe than the majority of other dances at their first opening. "The Soldier's Joy" has, too, an additional charm, in being so admirably adapted to the tambourine aforesaid—no mean instrument in the hands of a performer who understands the proper convulsions, spasms, St. Vitus's dances, and fearful frenzies necessary when exhibiting its tones in their highest perfection.

In rural England in the nineteenth century, the attraction of "The Soldier's Joy" is its capacity to support dancing. At the farm dance described by Hardy, its expressiveness is not the point.

If we could go back in time and interview the anonymous composer of this reel, we would probably discover a Scottish fiddler. He might confirm my hunch that expressiveness was never the point. The three fiddlers at Weatherbury farm must have been exhausted—and perhaps bored, too—after playing the same reel for forty-five minutes. Perhaps the composer of "The Soldier's Joy" was simply very bored of playing whatever reel was then popular in the Scottish highlands, and wanted something new to play at dances. Perhaps he just wanted to show off his musical skills. However, in creating a new reel, he also created something with a joyful expressive character.

As a general rule, a reel has a lively tempo in common time, with a heavy emphasis on the downbeat. Reels are commonly played with a bit of lilt, which is created by playing the downbeats a fraction early, in front of the anticipated beat. Although some reels are associated with sad titles and texts, such as "The Hangman's Reel" (in French-Canada, "Le Reel du pendu"), they are inherently happy-sounding. I defer to Scottish poet Robert Fergusson:

> For nought can cheer the heart [so well]
> As can a canty Highland reel.
> It even vivifies the heel
> To skip and dance:
> Lifeless is he wha canna feel
> Its influence.

So I challenge anyone to write a decent medium tempo or up-tempo reel with a Highland rhythm that is expressively sad. Given the inherent tendency of such reels to sound happy, the "happiness" of "The Soldier's Joy" is no reason to conclude that the expression of happiness was an element of the compositional process. Because its social purpose in that society at that time placed limits on the composer's creative process, and those cultural limitations directed it expressively, then some highly expressive music is expressive without being the expression of emotion.

III. THE SONG THRUSH

In the last section I argued that the presence of the expressive quality of happiness in a Scottish reel is adequately explained by noting that it was created as an instrumental tune to support a particular kind of dancing. In turn, it follows that it is simply wrong to think that expressive qualities of music are always present as an expression of emotion.

My argument collapses if we assume that certain musical patterns are just like facial expressions. On this assumption, certain musical patterns are the natural, universal expressions of our basic simple emotions. Someone who is sufficiently aware of these patterns might choose to actively suppress personal expression, creating emotionally neutral music, the way that adult Japanese often suppress facial expressions. Or she might use the patterns to generate insincere expressions of emotion. But if a composer does not actively avoid expressing her own emotions, her musical compositions will employ patterns that express her emotions. Or, recognizing that the extended time required to compose music makes it unlikely that a piece of music expresses an occurrent mental state, the advocate of natural expression might endorse William Wordsworth's proposal that poetry arises at a later time, as "the spontaneous overflow of powerful feelings: it takes its origin from emotion recollected in tranquility."

On this revised account, "'The Soldier's Joy' is joyful" means that the music reflects its composer's recollection of some earlier happy occasion or the composer had a miserable life but knew how to be insincere. Fans of Ludwig van Beethoven's "Pastoral" symphony (Op. 68) will point out how neatly this model fits Beethoven's program for his "Recollections of Country Life" and its warning that it is "more an expression of feeling than painting." Thus, the goal of Beethoven's first movement is to express "the awakening of cheerful feelings upon arriving in the country." Although I grant that Beethoven aimed at genuine expression in the sixth symphony, there are serious reasons to resist generalizing from the musical practices of nineteenth-century Vienna. It is a historically recent use of music. Projecting it back onto pre-modern music would be like thinking that the mourning garb of Victorian England is a natural response to death that was somehow repressed for all those preceding centuries. I will expand this objection in this chapter's final section. Until then, I will discuss more obvious problems with attributions of expression.

If the presence of distinctive patterns justifies the attribution of joy to music, then there is no reason to stop with music. If this position is supposed to provide a general account of the expressive qualities of music, then it should be applied to all expressive qualities. We are justified in assigning a capacity for emotional response wherever we find patterns that "naturally" convey emotive expressiveness. But that invites endless, unjustified anthropomorphism about the world around us. Our tendency toward anthropomorphic perception invites further scrutiny of seemingly expressive non-human music: the "music" of birds. Perhaps birds make joyful-sounding vocalizations for some non-expressive reason.

The heart of the argument is that music is not the only realm of experience that inspires application of the names of basic emotions to non-sentient things. Spontaneous anthropomorphism, the attribution of human characteristics to non-human objects and events, is a basic strategy that we use for locating patterns in complex perceptual information. We engage in a mild anthropomorphism when we say that our car "refuses" to start on a cold morning, that the weather isn't "cooperating" when it rains during our weekend at the lake, and that the stock market is "nervous." From a scientific perspective, the Ojibwa people of central North America engage in a strong anthropomorphism when educated members of the tribe endorse the traditional belief that the four winds are living creatures and that thunder and lightning are the observable effects of the thunder birds, persons with avian form, traveling through the air.

Activities that unfold in time are strong targets of anthropomorphism. Activity suggests life, encouraging anthropomorphic perception of non-human forms as embodiments of purposeful activity. Since the detection of emotion is central to our perception of human agency, it is not surprising to find that basic emotions are routinely attributed to musical patterns that unfold in time. This would happen even if no music were ever used to express emotion. And it is not that music is particularly begging to be treated in this way (itself an anthropomorphism). Steven Feld notes that the Kaluli people typically describe musical patterns as waterfalls, pools of water, and other water phenomena. If that same metaphor was widely used in Western musical aesthetics, we might think about "The Soldier's Joy" as a bubbling hot spring, totally side-stepping the question of what emotion it expresses.

Here we have our troubling double standard. Although scientifically literate people routinely use emotive vocabulary for cars, household appliances, the weather, and a host of other things, most of us have abandoned the theory that a "sad" willow tree and an "angry" rain squall express the emotions of some sentient agent. "Sad" music confronts us with an interesting problem concerning a widespread habit of thought and language, not a problem that is specific to music. The widespread belief that music is a special case is largely due to the continuing influence of a nineteenth-century Romantic aesthetic. I expand on this point in the final section of this chapter and then again in Chapter 4.

My position faces the obvious objection that music just happens to be a very special case. Granted, it's a mistake to think that the weather is a person with human-like emotions. However, birds express themselves musically. Therefore their activity is independent evidence for the thesis that music is a natural method for expressing emotion, and therefore we are dealing with a very different phenomenon than people who say that the stock market is nervous.

My argument against this special pleading for music is another appeal to our tendency to anthropomorphize what we perceive. Animals are so-named because they are animate, self-moving, and so we find it very difficult to avoid assigning them "inner" psychological states and motivations that parallel our own. My quarrel is not with the idea that birds, reptiles, and non-human mammals have mental states, including emotions. I am quite confident that my dog is emotionally frightened by the sound of thunder and is happy when I return home from a trip. I have no quarrel with the idea that monogamous birds feel differently about their mates than about other birds. My objection is based on the obvious point that non-human species do not, for the most part, express their emotions in the manner of humans. I am hardly the first person to say that if you want to know if a Saint Bernard is feeling happy, its facial "expression" is irrelevant. All Saint Bernards have sad-looking faces. That is, they are sad-looking by human standards. But dogs don't express happiness and sadness with facial expressions. They express emotion in their tails, stance, and mode of movement. If you're looking at their faces, you're falsely anthropomorphizing them. This warning is not specific to dogs. We cannot determine how any non-human species displays an occurrent emotion without carefully studying its patterns of behavioral response to different stimuli.

My argument against a universal, natural, cross-species proclivity to use music to express emotion is therefore quite simple. If you believe that Kaluli engage in anthropomorphism when they attribute grieving human souls to fruitdoves, then you should agree with me that the fruitdove's sad song is not a symptom of genuine sadness. Granted, the song of the fruitdove sounds sad to human perceivers.

But there is no more reason to think that fruitdoves are routinely sad and express that sadness with their songs than to think that Saint Bernards are naturally sad and express it with their faces. Since we cannot reliably determine how a dog feels by looking at its face, then we cannot reliably determine how a song thrush or a fruitdove feels by listening to its song. A "mournful" or "joyful" birdsong means no more than a "sad" dog's face. Until we have very good evidence otherwise, the expressive quality of a bird song is like the expressive quality of a Saint Bernard's face. We should resist anthropomorphic perception as a guide to their respective emotional states.

Rothenberg's appeal to the beauty of birdsong is subject to the same censure. Peacocks cannot see most of the colors in the male peacock's elaborate tail, and the male peacock's horrible screaming may well be more beautiful than their tails to females of the species. Our sense of beauty may be very different from theirs.

We should be equally cautious about using familiar cultural practices as a basis for making conclusions about the "natural" proclivities of our own species. The fact that it became all the rage to express emotion in instrumental music in nineteenth-century Europe is no reason to think that music was, from the dawn of our evolutionary history, our natural tool for expressing emotion. We are so accustomed to the thesis that art has the function of expressing the emotions of artists that it can be very difficult to acknowledge that the idea is of recent vintage. Informed appreciation of Beethoven's "Pastoral" symphony should acknowledge that it reflects the composer's recollected feelings. But it doesn't follow that the same holds for "The Soldier's Joy."

Until now, I have focused on the thesis that expressive-sounding music expresses emotion by making someone's emotion outwardly apparent. I have mentioned that this theory is of recent European origin. In contrast, the earliest Greek philosophers emphasize a different dimension of the expressive qualities of music. For example, when Plato discusses musical expression, he is far less concerned with the composer's externalization of feeling than with the listener's internalization of the music's expressive quality. Naturally sorrowful musical modes should be banished from the state, for they make us self-indulgent, weak, and prone to feel sad in the presence of misfortune. The Confucian tradition of Chinese philosophy also warns about music's expressive capacity and its attractions. Unlike Plato, Confucianism emphasizes a complete reciprocity between expression and reception. If musical choices reflect inner states, then hearing music will shape and control the inner states of listeners. Both Plato and Confucius conclude that the good of society demands censoring music that supports socially destructive emotions.

The thesis that sorrowful music makes listeners sorrowful and angry music makes them angry is logically independent of the idea that "'The Soldier's Joy' is joyful" attributes joy to its composer. Instead, the music is joyful in the same way that an overcast day is gloomy, that is, as a cause of that emotional state in observers. As you may already have noted about Robert Fergusson's praise of the Scottish reel, he endorses the reel as a superior cause of joy. We literally *feel* its influence. This theory about the meaning of "is joyful" in "the music is joyful" is traditionally known as the arousal theory, on the grounds that "is joyful" can be cashed out as meaning "arouses joy." Arousal theory comes in two versions. The first, less plausible version holds that expressive descriptions indicate that the speaker is reporting his or her own response. The second version denies that "the music is sad" is necessarily a first-person report. However, neither version is attractive as a general theory, for there are many situations in which neither version captures what we are communicating when we expressively label music.

The first-person version might capture what some people mean when they talk about sad and joyful music, but it falls apart when we consider people who have something more to say than "it makes me sad." Consider boredom, an emotion that I have mentioned only in passing. Suppose Professor Harmonious teaches music appreciation and she asks her students, "What did you think of 'Trio,' by King Crimson?" "It was peaceful," one says. "It was boring," another responds. It is plausible that the first student is reporting that the music had a calming effect and the second is reporting that it caused boredom. The difficulty is that, if Professor Harmonious continues the discussion and asks the second student whether the first student's description is appropriate, the second student might very well endorse it. An individual can be bored to tears by a piece of music and yet know perfectly well that it is not expressing boredom. (There is nothing special about boredom. Annoyance is another emotion. I know people who find country music very annoying and yet who have no difficulty distinguishing between sad tunes, happy ones, humorous ones, and so on.)

To deal with the objection that the bored student is not reporting her own peacefulness, a second version of the arousal theory is available to preserve the theory's core insight. When she agrees that "Trio" is peaceful, she is saying that the

On Music

music typically or frequently produces a peaceful feeling in listeners. I will grant that this analysis captures what some speakers intend to communicate on some occasions, as when a record label packages music together as *The Most Relaxing Classical Music in the Universe*. It is a prediction that it will relax people. However, as a general account of what it means to say that a piece of music "is sad" or "is joyful," this analysis fails on the grounds that it requires us to overlook much of the evidence that we have about music's typical tendencies to arouse listeners. When it is not in actual conflict with our real estimation of the effects of listening to a particular piece of music, it reflects unjustified speculation. For example, if you listen to King Crimson's "Trio" on the *Starless and Bible Black* album and to "Blue in Green" on the Miles Davis *Kind of Blue* album, and you find them boring, as a very great many listeners do, then what is your evidence for their calming effect on others? If you actually go looking for that evidence, I wager that you will discover that these two pieces of music bore most people—most people are not fans of these styles of music and are quickly bored by the placidity of these two pieces. If one needs another example, "amusing" appears to be a solid candidate for the revised arousal theory, as a label that indicates an expectation that a piece of music will amuse most people. Wolfgang Amadeus Mozart's *Ein musikalischer Spaß* (K. 522, "A Musical Joke") and Led Zeppelin's "D'yer Mak'er" are two highly amusing pieces of music, but I say this with full knowledge that nine out of ten randomly chosen people will not hear the musical jokes.

To summarize the two great difficulties for arousal theory, many people assign expressive labels that do not reflect their personal response and without waiting to observe how others actually respond to it. However, if neither personal response nor general pattern of response is consulted in order to assign joyfulness to music, then the music itself must display an aural property that is appropriately described as "joyful." The joyfulness of "The Soldier's Joy" must be a property that emerges from its musical structure. Applied to music, an expressive label is a description of an emergent, gestalt property that the particular piece of music shares with other music that is described with the same term. It is like seeing that a vase has a fragile design without having to break it. On that basis the music may be predicted to be the source of emotional contagion for some listeners, or regarded as a suitable vehicle for self-expression if used in that way. However, theorizing that music's expressive qualities are essentially bound to these functional uses of music is to let the tail wag the dog.

Some defenders of arousal theory will respond that I am being unfair, because I am ignoring basic ideas that I defended in the last chapter. Ignorant listening is not relevant. The responses that matter are those of listeners with sufficient familiarity to grasp the relevant musical structures. Most people have not acquired the right concepts for hearing what's funny in Mozart's "A Musical Joke," and I have argued elsewhere that what is amusing about the Led Zeppelin piece is equally dependent on the right mix of musical and cultural information. The proper question, therefore, is whether informed listeners have the responses required by either version of arousal theory. My response has two prongs. First, if arousal theory is supposed to account for the natural expressiveness of sound, then the test group should be randomly selected people, drawn from people who listen to all sorts of music. Focusing on the responses of culturally informed audiences would be as misleading as demonstrating that there is a "natural" and universal sense of justice by questioning college graduates in the United States. Second, if we are going to defend arousal theory while abandoning the theory of natural expressiveness, then we introduce several new problems. For example, there is the problem of audiences who respond with "been-there, done-that, no-longer-interesting." In other words, well-informed respondents are generally able to identify the emotional tone of a piece of music based on very little information. Then recall Brahms's famous insult ("Every jackass hears that!") when he wanted to make the point that what's obvious about a piece of music is unlikely to be what's musically interesting in it. Informed listeners frequently regard the music's expressivity as a mere starting point for appreciation. They are generally more interested in the musical skill displayed in the composing and performing than in the act of expressing emotion. Eduard Hanslick appears to have been on the right track: if expression is elemental in music, it will be the same thing, over and over, and it will not sustain the aesthetic interest of more informed listeners.

V. KALULI GRIEF, AMERICAN JAZZ, HINDUSTANI RASA

For the remainder of this chapter I return to the topic of music as art. For the sake of argument, suppose that there is a pure, original music and that three things are true about it. Suppose that we have some natural proclivity to perceive basic expressive qualities in many things, including musical patterns. (Many theorists push the story back a step and say that the true origin is the expressivity of vocal tones, which is then developed into music.) Suppose that, as a general rule, expressive musical patterns originate in the emotional lives of those who create those patterns. And suppose that, as a general rule, listeners respond to those patterns by experiencing, either genuinely or imaginatively, the emotions that are expressed. We now have a theory of why "The Soldier's Joy" exhibits joy and we have an account of why there is such a strong consensus that it is joyful. However, we are not yet making any connection between expressivity and art. Therefore it is seriously misleading to point to a beautiful and "expressive" bird song and identify it as a species of musical art. Exhibiting symptoms is different from creating art.

The most telling difference between exhibiting an emotion and artistically expressing it is that art invites appreciation. Appreciation is different from mere liking or admiration. It is a complex evaluation of a human achievement within a particular tradition. In Chapter 2, I mentioned the Beatles' "In My Life." Liking the "harpsichord" sound is a much simpler response than appreciating its studio virtuosity. To clarify my argument, let's consider a seemingly simple case of appreciating a musical performance.

Let's return to Feld's fieldwork in Papua New Guinea. Although Kaluli explain their use of the grieving weeping-into-song by pointing to its origins in the song of the fruitdove, Feld reports their interest in the recordings that he made of particular rituals. He was intrigued by the fact that many members of the village visited his house in order to request playback of a specific improvisation, in which a woman, Hane, addresses the spirit of Bibiali, a male cousin. The improvised song lasts just under five minutes. Why, Feld wondered, did so many people want to hear that particular song? As Feld interviewed people who sought out the recording, he found that they were drawn to its aesthetic achievement: "Kaluli found its construction controlled, deliberate, crafted, and almost composed like a song."

Although improvised, it was a strikingly superior articulation of grief. In other words, Kaluli do not treat all musical self-expression as equally valuable natural expressions. They listen for, and appreciate, the artistry of coherent articulation "within the constraints of an improvised form." In short, Kaluli apply standards to Hane's public grieving that are not applied to non-artistic expression of grief. Kaluli admire Hane's performance in much the way that jazz fans applaud some performances of "Goodbye Pork Pie Hat," Charles Mingus's music to commemorate Lester Young, as aesthetically better than others.

Kaluli admiration of Hane's song of grief is strikingly like the European Romantic preference for expressive specificity and particularization. However, artistic individualization is a criterion for *artistic* success that we do not apply to natural outpouring of basic emotion. When people praise the expressive improvisations of Hane and jazz musicians as direct and spontaneous outpourings of pure feeling that they cannot contain, the evaluation is condescending. Ted Gioia points out that aesthetic admiration of "primitive," natural self-expression is a mainstay of jazz criticism. Yet what it really does, he notes, is treat the musician as "practitioner of an art which he himself scarcely understands. . . . Presented in such terms, the jazz performance seems hardly a cultural event and more like a medical affliction, akin to epilepsy." An aesthetic evaluation of someone's epileptic seizure objectifies and dehumanizes them. Evaluating Hane's highly expressive music as an uncontrolled symptom of emotion is no better.

However, I must caution against generalizing too widely from the examples of Hane's song and jazz improvisation. Both examples conform to expectations about musical expression that are associated with the European Romantic account of art. Earlier in this chapter, I quoted Wordsworth's influential formulation about expressive poetry. Romantic ideals continue to influence art. As Jenefer Robinson points out, a generic "smiley face" has an expressive quality, but that does not make it an expression of emotion in the Romantic sense. The Romantic aesthetic endorses a high degree of individuation of emotion. Artistic expression is valuable when it precisely articulates a unique version of an emotion. Even when the emotions are those of a fictional character who is clearly not the artist, as in Bob Dylan's "North Country Blues," the expressivity is expected to reveal something new about the human capacity for emotion. Robinson observes that Romantic expression requires more than skilled making, for artistic expression requires the articulation "of new and unique emotional states." Whether we find it in Kaluli appreciation of Hane's song or in English poet Philip Larkin's appreciation of Mingus, Romantic expression places a high value on the individuality of each person.

More importantly, assigning a shared criterion for success to Hane and Mingus assumes that personal expression is a functionally distinctive approach to expressive qualities of artworks. Appreciating the expressivity of a particular piece of music requires appreciating choices made against the background of musical and therefore cultural constraint. But we can also step back from the particular case and appreciate the tradition as an evolving collective choice to endorse expressive art. That choice is subject to revision. There would be no point to identifying and debating the Romantic theory of expression if it was the only game in town. Romantic expression is a cultural preference, not a musical universal. Some traditions endorse high levels of musical individualization without interpreting it as unique, personal expression.

In Chapter 2, I discussed audience confusion about the categories of tuning and performing at the start of Ravi Shankar's performance during the 1971 benefit concert for Bangladesh. That mistake was easily corrected by Shankar's joke, for the audience already possessed (but had incorrectly applied) the concept of performance. However, it is considerably more difficult to appreciate the expressivity of Hindustani classical music correctly, because it *rejects* the core value of Romantic expression theory. It questions the individuality of each person. The goal of musical performance is to exhibit *rasa*, which is a refined, de-personalized exhibition of the flavor of a basic emotion. When Shankar engages in an extended improvisation of a classic raga, his artistic goal is completely distorted by approaching the performance as personal expression. Nor is it offered as mere musical virtuosity. The Hindustani aesthetics sees nothing valuable about pure, expressionless music. Technical skill has a spiritual purpose. Standard Western interpretations, Shankar warns, are simply *wrong*.

Most Westerners cannot formulate—or, upon having it explained, cannot take seriously—the philosophical doctrine that individuality is a problem in need of a solution and part of the solution is to purge it from music. Although the point is often ignored by secular musicians and audiences in India, Hindustani classical art reflects the view that art is a path to enlightenment. In Hinduism, enlightenment is an escape from the "self" that loves, hates, suffers, and laughs. The central aesthetic principle of Hindustani art, Raj Kumar explains, is the presentation of impersonal, universalized emotion, so "the final effect that is left on [audience members] is not that of the passion depicted but is an impersonal absorption in the aesthetic mood." Artistic expressivity is highly valued as a method of purging personal emotions. In this tradition, instrumental music displays *rasa* rather than *bhāva*. Crudely summarized, *bhāvas* are mental states, including the important subset of *sthāyibhāvas*, the basic emotions. Sorrow and anger are *sthāyibhāvas*. Their display is common in representational art. Michelangelo's *Pietà* displays the *bhāva* of sorrow and it may arouse empathetic sorrow in viewers. But that is a superficial first step for the viewer.

Each of the basic emotions has a corresponding *rasa* (literally, "sap" or an extract or flavor that we can taste and savor). The point of listening to music is to "taste" its *rasa*. However, a *rasa* is not a *bhāva*. The difference is sometimes expressed with the metaphor that *bhāva* is to *rasa* as grapes are to wine. Hindustani aesthetics highlights the distinction between *bhāva* and *rasa* by assigning them different names. Sorrow (*shoka*) is an emotion, but its *rasa* is pathos (*karuna*). Although it is rarely found in music, the emotion of disgust (*jugupsā*) is allied with a rasa of repulsiveness (*bābhatsa*). More than four dozen *bhāvas* are recognized in Hindustani aesthetics, but only nine *rasas*.

However "expressively" complex a work might be in representing emotion, the real goal of art is to present the audience with a single, unified *rasa*. Established musical structures are merely blueprints. Music is energy, and so the musician must energize the melodic framework. To present *rasa*, Shankar explains, "The musician must breathe life" into the melody, "mak[ing] the bare notes vibrate, pulsate, come alive." From a Western or Kaluli perspective, the resulting particularity of one of Shankar's performances might appear to be his expression of a unique and personalized emotion. However, to "appreciate" it in that manner is to admire it without taking an interest in the performance's true goal. Transcendence requires a skilled performer to extract and present a rarefied essence of an emotion, rather than mere self-expression.

We can tell all the stories we like about the natural evolutionary sources of music as an account of music's expressive potentials. However, we must also recognize the difference between Jaco Pastorius's gesture in opening his debut album with "Donna Lee" and Ravi Shankar's aim of revealing the essence of erotic-romantic longing when he performs *Raga Bhimpalasi*. Unlike Shankar but like Hane, Pastorius was engaged in self-expression. In Chapter 1, I explained how Pastorius's expressive gesture depends on its place in a musical tradition. He relies on cultural norms and expectations *about music*. When music is used as Romantic expression of a highly individualized emotion, that functional use relies on cultural expectation that does not apply to Shankar's performances of traditional music. The contrast between Hindustani and "Romantic" improvisation illustrates that the expressive function of art does not lie in a universal human proclivity to use music in just one way. There are multiple musical arts with distinct expressive functions. Knowing which function is present in a performance requires a judgment about the music's origins in a particular system of symbolic interactions and social preferences.

We can go one more step in the analysis. Individual composers and musicians can deploy expressive qualities in different ways on different occasions. Pastorius's fretless electric bass is the musical highlight of one of my favorite records, Joni Mitchell's *Hejira*. (Like *Jaco Pastorius*, *Hejira* was released in 1976.) Although his contribution is crucial to *Hejira's* power, Pastorius is supporting Mitchell's expressive gestures. His own emotions are not the point. So his musical exploration of emotion is functionally different from the personal gesture of arranging "Donna Lee." The *Hejira* performances are more like Shankar's relationship to *Raga Bhimpalasi*. Conversely, Shankar spent part of his childhood in Paris and a good deal of the middle period of his musical career working with non-Indian musicians. No stranger to Western music, Shankar's three concertos for sitar and Western orchestra are, I suggest, best approached as his personal expressions of pride in his Indian heritage. Again, music is art because its meaning is inseparable from its cultural contexts.

Four

> The art of music is sublime because, not having the means to imitate what is real, it ascends beyond common nature into a world that is ideal, and with its celestial harmony it has the power to move earthly passions.
>
> (Gioachino Rossini)

> The greatness of German music appeals to the sublimity of spiritual forms.
>
> (Jacques Derrida)

Musical encounters can be life-defining events. Bound for Mexico and a reunion with her husband and children, Baroness Pannonica de Koenigswarter was headed for the airport when she detoured to the apartment of a friend, jazz pianist Teddy Wilson. In the course of their conversation, Wilson mentioned a relatively obscure jazz pianist, Thelonious Monk. She'd never heard the name. Knowing de Koenigswarter's taste in jazz, Wilson insisted on playing Monk's recording of "'Round Midnight." (Several composers got their names on the copyright, but the tune is Monk's. Lovingly called the national anthem of jazz, it now stands as the most recorded piece ever composed by a jazz musician.) Many of Monk's compositions are angular, spiky, and dissonant. In a few spots, so is "'Round Midnight." But the primary theme evokes a wistful, late-night mood. Hearing it for the first time, de Koenigswarter cried. She later said that she was so enraptured by it that she played it twenty times consecutively. That might be an exaggeration of memory, but it might be near the truth. She did not continue her cab ride to the airport. Instead, she took it to a New York hotel. As she interpreted "'Round Midnight," the instrumental composition presented a vision of freedom that empowered her to reject all of the social expectations and constraints that had shaped the first four decades of her life. As a result of her chance encounter with three minutes of music, de Koenigswarter abandoned her husband and five children. She was determined to devote the remainder of her life to jazz and the company of jazz musicians. When she finally got the chance to watch Thelonious Monk perform, three years later, that experience led her to further reorganize her life. For nearly three decades, she supported Monk in any way she could. Often, this meant serving as his chauffeur when he had a gig in or near New York. Once, she risked imprisonment when she protected him by falsely confessing to a drug possession charge when he was the guilty party.

While this response to music is extreme, stories about music's life-altering powers date back to the dawn of human record keeping. In *The Odyssey*, music is so intoxicating that it is life-threatening. In Book XII, Odysseus encounters the sirens, whose songs and singing are so enchanting that men will pilot their ships into the corpse-strewn rocks and die in order to hear them. In the Judeo-Christian tradition, the blowing of seven horns was sufficient to collapse the walls of Jericho. The inhabitants were massacred. Other traditions regard music as fundamentally beneficial. Hindu tradition regards music as a gift of the gods, given to the sage Narada ("Knowledge-Giver") in order to generate greater peace and cooperation among humans. Moreover, music is a path to spiritual liberation. Hindu theology regards melodic chanting of sacred texts as the primary mode of access to the divine, for at root the cosmos is primordial music. Human music that echoes the primordial music can bring enlightenment. While the Judeo-Christian tradition does not elevate music to that level, its spiritual power is significant. In the first book of Samuel, harp music frees Saul from the torments of an evil spirit.

The sacred connection is neither a relic of history nor a curiosity of non-Western cultures. It remains a core conviction of many music lovers. For example, consider the prominence of the topic in the documentary film, *They Came to Play*, which chronicles the fortunes of competitors at the 2007 Van Cliburn Piano Competition for Outstanding Amateurs. The contest is restricted to adults above the age of thirty-five. The film follows a diverse group of amateur pianists, including a doctor, a lawyer, a jewelry designer, a dental assistant, a financial planner, a retired physicist from Berlin, and a retired tennis coach from Paris. Asked to explain their devotion to music, three of the profiled competitors insist that their musical ability is a divine gift and that musical performance is a religious or spiritual practice. Kent Lietzau, a military procurement planner whose other hobby is flying, enjoys playing the ragtime music of Scott Joplin. Music, Lietzau says, is a glimpse of a part of God. While I have never personally responded to Scott Joplin's music in this way, I think it is a mistake to dismiss this response too quickly. Because it is an important dimension of music for many people in many cultures, it deserves serious consideration. At the same time, I am not ready to endorse the wide spectrum of spiritual interpretations that have been placed on music.

I. INEFFABLE REALITIES

Music's capacity to reveal the sacred or divine is not necessarily related to God. William James once put it this way: "Music gives us ontological messages which non-musical criticism is unable to contradict, though it may laugh at our foolishness in minding them." James endorsed its capacity to disclose "a more spiritual universe." We should also remain mindful of the fact that music's special relationship to spirituality is prized by traditions that do not emphasize its capacity to reveal God or gods. The classical music and dance tradition of India is closely associated with Hinduism. Yet this route to enlightenment is not a path to deities. The ideal music, Ravi Shankar claims, is "a kind of spiritual discipline that raises one's inner being to divine peacefulness and bliss." Divine peacefulness is not ordinary peacefulness. It is not the peace of mind that comes from escaping the daily grind by sipping tropical drinks at a beach resort. Likewise, it is not the mood created by playing *Mozart for Relaxation* as background music. To generate *divine* peacefulness and bliss, music must instill awareness of aspects of reality that are, by definition, other than ordinary. If this process involves emotion, as Shankar assumes, then the music must do something more than express or arouse ordinary human emotions. Suppose there is an element of truth in the Hindu tradition that Shankar promotes. If so, the path to spiritual insight requires something more than ordinary expressiveness.

Furthermore, I will not address music that promotes particular religions and their theologies. Olivier Messiaen's *Quatuor pour la fin du temps* (Quartet for the End of Time) is a programmatic chamber work inspired by specific passages in the New Testament's Book of Revelation. Although he composed and first performed the work while a prisoner of war in a German *Stalag* during the Second World War, Messiaen was not expressing a personal vision of the divine. He understood that he was crafting musical symbols to convey particular theological truths of the Roman Catholic faith. As such, his quartet stands in the same tradition as G.W.F. Handel's *Messiah* and Joseph Haydn's *The Creation*. In all these cases, the music's spirituality is a byproduct of its composer's overt intention to support Christianity. It is accomplished through the incorporation of religious texts or, for instrumental music, through programmatic links to religious texts and theological doctrines. But this method of inserting the divine into music is a piggy-backing of religion on to music. Such music cannot count as evidence that *music* has a capacity to reach what is divine or spiritual. Anyone who is not already inclined to interpret it as spiritual will see it as nothing more than music put to a spiritual purpose, in the same way that Woody Guthrie's "Union Maid" has a political purpose because it has political lyrics. Guthrie could have used the same tune for a children's song, like his "(Take Me) Riding in My Car." However, if that is how Messiaen's Quartet is spiritual, by programmatic or textual piggy-backing, then an external agenda imparts spirituality to what might equally well be profane. In the case of Handel's *Messiah*, this charge is literally true. Handel composed much of the music for romantic Italian songs and then recycled it as religious music many years later.

Having set aside standard uses of music to express emotion as well as texts, extra-musical narrative, and the presentation of religious doctrines, what's left for us to discuss? Historically, we are in good company if we say that music can be especially potent due to its capacity to reveal the mystical without the interpretive support of religious doctrines or descriptive programs. Some music conveys the divine by putting us in touch with what is otherwise ineffable, nameless, and beyond the descriptive capacity of language.

From the ancient Hindu Upanishads to the Islamic philosopher Ibn al-Tufail to Catholic medieval mystic St Catherine of Siena, there is agreement that a genuine spiritual vision is so sublime and unique that the tongue cannot describe it. Yet the *desire* to tell about it is inevitable. Music, it is frequently thought, can offer a way around the limitations of descriptive language. Ludwig Wittgenstein is famous for a number of aphorisms. One is, "There is indeed the inexpressible in speech. This *shows* itself; it is the mystical." And, "Whereof one cannot speak, thereof one must be silent." This pair of remarks opposes speaking and showing. Speaking revolves around our capacity for description and using language to express propositions that are either true or false. Taken together, Wittgenstein's two remarks underscore the basic problem that faces the mystical tradition. When we try to explain the mystical, we simply talk nonsense. If we want to communicate it, we need a different communicative strategy. Perhaps music, which is not speech, can break the silence in a way that shows the mystical. Perhaps a composer can design music that directs us to the thing that shows itself, but which we otherwise might not perceive. If we can substantiate music's capacity to show the mystical and the ineffable, then I am certainly ready to endorse music's revelatory connection with spirituality.

The ineffable is not necessarily a hidden plane of reality. For Wittgenstein, the mystical is simply "things that cannot be put into words." For him, the mystical appears to include a great deal, including all absolute moral values. Jean-François Lyotard proposes that the problem of representing the unrepresentable also arises in the attempt to convey the significance of the Holocaust and other large-scale human atrocities. He offers the writing of James Joyce as an example of literature that "searches for new presentations, not in order to enjoy them but in order to impart a stronger sense of the unrepresentable." Wittgenstein seems to have thought, similarly, that the mystical can only be conveyed through unparaphrasable similes. For composers and performers, the parallel challenge is to communicate something that is normally invisible or incomprehensible—something that cannot be put into words because it escapes conceptual categorization and recognition—without relying on words to allude to it. But without words, there is no simile. Perhaps Kiene Wurth is on the right track in emphasizing that the paradox is that we are seeking occasions of insight that arise from experiential rupture and displacement—the qualities that Pannonica de Koenigswarter interpreted as freedom in Monk's "'Round Midnight." Wurth notes that such ruptures are "inextricably intertwined with the forms, bounds, and contexts" of ordinary experiences. A rupture is only a rupture when it is understood in contrast to an established sense of the everyday, the profane, and the normal. However, this strategy is equally available to architecture, painting, poetry, and other media. It does not support the intuition that music is an especially potent path to the mystical or the divine, which is my goal in this chapter.

Having selected the ineffable as a criterion of spirituality, I caution that mere ineffability is not sufficient. An experience of ineffability is just a starting point for thinking that we have a potential candidate for the mystical. We must take care to distinguish between two species of musical ineffability.

1   We are unable to describe what music is doing to us when we hear it, because many features of music do not fall within the scope of what language can describe.
2   We are unable to offer a verbal paraphrase of what music communicates when what it communicates is beyond the capacity of language. For example, this happens when music is a conduit to something divine, transcendental, or supernatural.

We should resist the temptation to think that the first kind of ineffability demonstrates that the second kind is also present. Veterans of military combat generally regard its horrors as ineffable, beyond description. But they do not generally regard combat as a spiritual realm. What is worse, ineffability is not reserved for special cases such as combat. This first kind of ineffability, Stephen Davies observes, is present in almost every human experience. Experience is more fine-grained than language. Suppose that we are having dinner together and I order steamed mussels. I offer you a taste but you decline because you have a shellfish allergy. You ask me to describe the taste. How far will I get? However refined my palate and broad my culinary vocabulary, I will provide a rather shallow description. Most of the experience is inexpressible. Musical ineffability gets us nowhere if, as Davies argues, "the ineffability of music is a result of the ineffability of all sensory experience."

If Monk's "'Round Midnight" is ineffable for precisely the same reason that the smell of new-mown grass and the taste of cod liver oil are ineffable, then music's ineffability is not a positive value for music and not a reason to listen to it. As a matter of fact, I think Davies is correct that ineffability arises for the basic qualia of experience and therefore of many aspects of musical experience. Therefore I conclude that mere ineffability does not demonstrate a "divine" connection. We need more than music's own ineffability to substantiate the claim that music is ineffable in the second way: ineffable because it maps or pictures or directs us to something external to the music that is *significantly* ineffable. The remainder of this chapter makes the case that musical sublimity is the best candidate for creating the conditions for this second species of ineffability.

I must add a word of caution. In examining a certain kind of musical sublimity, I am merely offering it as an exemplary case of music's spiritual dimension. I am not suggesting that my remarks about exemplification will account for the whole range of musical examples that are considered to be spiritual. I am not even saying that my account applies to all music that listeners regard as sublime. However, there seems to be an important experience of sublimity that does not depend on textual prompts or programmatic guidance, yet which is appropriately understood as informative about a broader range of sublime ineffability.

II. THE BEAUTIFUL GIVES WAY TO THE SUBLIME

The European tradition has promoted two distinct ideas about music's means of capturing what is otherwise ineffable. I summarized one of them in Chapter 1. It is the ancient tradition that the universe is filled with unheard music—one example is the music of the spheres—and that sound is organized musically when it conforms to the fundamental, divine ratios. If this correspondence is lacking, Augustine says, singing is merely "corporeal noise." However, I argued that this tradition was too conservative. Mathematics ruled music, rather than the ear, and therefore music theory limited what could be endorsed as musically beautiful. The extent of the problem became clear when the older model could not account for the attractions of instrumental music that developed in Europe at the end of the eighteenth century.

Ludwig van Beethoven was a particular affront to music theory. We now classify him as among the very greatest of composers. But I wager that many classical music lovers are not aware of the amount of critical hostility directed at Beethoven. Through much of the nineteenth century, many listeners and composers felt that the influence of his ugly, violent music was polluting what was beautiful and good in musical art. In order to defend Beethoven's music, his supporters turned to German philosophy of art and extracted an alternative standard for artistic success. Music does not have to be beautiful. Instead, it can be sublime. The two categories are characterized by distinctive aesthetic responses. Beauty evokes admiration and pleasure. The sublime incites awe and astonishment. There is admiration and pleasure and even exhilaration, but sublimity has a dark side, too. There is a sense of being overwhelmed, which is sometimes mingled with the pain of incomprehension or fear or terror. According to Friedrich von Schiller, there is a sudden sense of freedom. Many writers of the early modern period thought that sublimity was seldom found in art, for its paradigm examples were mountain ranges, volcanic eruptions, violent storms, and other overwhelming phenomena. Immanuel Kant, one of the key figures in the German tradition, had difficulty naming any sublime art beyond architecture, such as St Peter's Basilica in Rome.

By 1810, it was apparent to some philosophically informed music lovers that they could side-step criticism of Beethoven's music as undisciplined and ugly by re-classifying it as sublime. The best-known version of this position was presented by E.T.A. Hoffmann. Defending Beethoven's superiority over all other composers, Hoffmann argues that his mature "Romantic" style suppresses personal expression in favor of "siren voices . . . [that] work upon the human soul" with "the character of infinite longing." It is a siren call because the pleasure is mixed with pain: "Beethoven's music sets in motion the lever of fear, of awe, of horror, of suffering." There is beauty in his music, but it is often an "awesome beauty." Although Hoffmann seldom uses the word "sublime," it is the controlling idea in this passage:

> Beethoven's instrumental music opens up to us also the realm of the monstrous and the immeasurable. Burning flashes of light shoot through the deep night of this realm, and we become aware of giant shadows that surge back and forth, driving us into narrower and narrower confines until they destroy us—but . . . we live on, enchanted beholders of the supernatural.

A number of musicologists and historians have explored the cultural forces at work in Hoffmann's rhetoric. As a philosopher, that is not my main concern. I am concerned with the *plausibility* of the controlling concept, which is that music permits listeners to behold the ineffable. Since the late eighteenth and early nineteenth centuries, the sublime has been touted as a means by which music can achieve this goal.

The distinction between the beautiful and the sublime provides a partial explanation of why there is so much disagreement about particular cases. Pressed to name instrumental music that speaks to me with flashes of illumination in the darkness of the ineffable, I would nominate some of Dmitri Shostakovich's string quartets, some of the Grateful Dead's epic improvisations on their "Dark Star" theme, and Morton Feldman's *Rothko Chapel*. These are all, not coincidentally, music that satisfies the criteria for the sublime. But not everyone has a taste for the sublime. (What's more, some experiences characterized as sublime do not fit my proposed criteria, such as Edmund Burke's view that the experience always arises from terror.) I mentioned at the outset that I do not share Kent Lietzau's opinion that Scott Joplin's music offers a glimpse of the supernatural. In part, my hesitation derives from my preference for the sublime and my conviction that Joplin's rags, while thoroughly enchanting, are not sublime. I would wager that Lietzau is responding to the beauty of the music's interior logic. While a religious inclination makes it easy to see God in every beautiful artwork, the sublime reminds us that the God of Abraham is not all sweetness and light.

III. SCHOPENHAUER'S ACCOUNT OF MUSIC

I don't want to be too hasty in setting beauty aside. Many philosophers have connected musical beauty and ineffability. The most famous and compelling account was developed by Arthur Schopenhauer. His support for it includes arguments why alternative views fail. In this section, I explain and critique Schopenhauer's position. I think that he goes wrong in linking music's spiritual power to music's status as a universal language. Later in this chapter I respond by arguing that music's status as a cultural product does not undermine its revelatory capacity. It unleashes it.

Schopenhauer's theory is presented in *The World as Will and Representation*. Influenced by his reading of both Buddhism and the Hindu Upanishads, the third and final edition appeared in 1859. Admittedly, it is not read much anymore. Yet its influence on Western music is incalculable. From Franz Liszt through Arnold Schoenberg, Schopenhauer's position that music is a universal, metaphysically significant language was endorsed by many composers during the nineteenth century. These ideas gained new circulation in the early twentieth century when they were popularized in the writings of Rudolf Steiner. Approvingly citing the authority of Schopenhauer, Steiner writes, "If we are at all capable of experiencing a foretaste of the spiritual world, this would be found in the melodies and harmonies of music and the effects it has on the human soul."

Crudely summarized, Schopenhauer holds that the perceivable, phenomenal world is a superficial and distorting manifestation of reality. It does not matter whether you look at a towering redwood tree or at a heap of decaying garbage. Their obvious phenomenal differences are trivial. The division of the world into distinct things is a mask that objectifies an unperceived, unifying reality. Part of the problem, Schopenhauer warns, is that concepts and language are tools for making sense of the phenomenal world. They are tools or instruments for satisfying our desires. As such, they deal with the world from a limited perspective, suppressing the messy particularity of experience in order to view it from outside, from "without." Therefore the inner nature of the world is literally inexpressible, as a realm that cannot be grasped conceptually or described.

So are we merely prisoners of our own subjectivity? Fortunately, according to Schopenhauer, there is an escape route. There is music, especially pure instrumental music. He holds that music has a unique, "secret" ability to unveil the reality beyond the phenomenal world. When it is not governed by disfiguring concepts, musical flow is governed by an otherwise hidden activity. From a simple folk melody to a symphony, Schopenhauer contends that melodic form directly reflects the strivings of the universal Will. Schopenhauer's keen interest in Indian thought is the likely source for this linkage of melody, abstract emotion, and the strivings of the Will. (Contrary to the experiences of many people, Schopenhauer seems to hold that drumming cannot be revelatory.) Whenever a harmonized melody does its job properly, it conveys purified, abstract emotion. When it is not clouded by conceptual thought and language, melodic form has the power to provide a transcendent experience. Musical relationships are inherently revelatory, showing the reality behind the veil.

However, that means music, not mixed media. Music's revelatory function is sabotaged when words compete for our attention or when the music is not sufficiently melodic. The conceptual task of processing language takes our attention away from melody. Nonetheless, Schopenhauer allows that some songs succeed in taking us beyond the phenomenal world. A properly designed and highlighted melody can place sung words into a subordinate position in the listening experience. His examples include the operas of Gioachino Rossini and some musical settings of the Roman Catholic mass. The fact that the mass is in Latin, so that we do not attend to the words, helps to mitigate their presence. But, Rossini and the mass aside, symphonic music is best. However, none of this implies that all instrumental music opens the way to the mystical. A great deal of instrumental music fails because it is "imitative." It operates as a species of representation, "brought about with conscious intention by means of concepts." Schopenhauer points to the imitations of nature in Joseph

Haydn's *The Seasons*, which features the croaking of frogs and a raging summer storm. Today, I suspect that most people will be more familiar with similar techniques in Antonio Vivaldi's *The Four Seasons*, or the sounds of exploding bombs in Jimi Hendrix's Woodstock performance of "The Star Spangled Banner." My own favorite example is Mississippi John Hurt's use of acoustic guitar to imitate various train sounds when performing "Talking Casey." For Schopenhauer, auditory imitation in music ruins it by dividing our attention. As with most opera and song, the music fails because melody does not dominate the experience. The musical line is perverted by extra-musical phenomena. Concepts intrude into the experience, which is therefore grasped from outside. The listener is directed away from the ineffable, and the music's power to show without saying gives way to an ordinary, conceptually guided experience.

Schopenhauer's argument hinges on dividing music into two types. He thinks that a melody is either an unfiltered manifestation of the universal Will, and thus a glimpse into the inner nature of the world, or the music functions as a representation, the way that all other art functions, and it does not reveal the mystical. The common failing of music in this latter category—including songs, imitation, and programmatic associations—is that the sonic experience displays and therefore encourages conceptual thinking. On this view, Beethoven's Pastoral symphony and John Coltrane's *A Love Supreme* album are as earthbound and limited as any other "imitative" art. (Let's set aside the issue of whether these are all cases of imitation, and whether they always display conscious intention. Those are side issues.)

I have already explained why we should regard Schopenhauer's first, privileged category as an empty set. My first two chapters argued that all musical design reflects composers' and performers' conceptual understanding of music and its possibilities. The basic melodic patterns that constitute the raga system of Indian music do not sound particularly melodic to Western ears. Recall Eduard Hanslick's observation that all music is shot through with culture: "What we hear a Tyrolean peasant singing, into which seemingly no trace of art penetrates, is artistic music through and through." However, if there is no "pure" music that can be created and then appreciated without conceptual guidance, then music's capacity to communicate is no more universal than the other arts. So I reject Schopenhauer's argument for music's universal metaphysical significance. Music is art, and ignorance of its cultural and stylistic conventions shackles us.

A final criticism of Schopenhauer's theory is that he does not endorse sublimity in pure instrumental music. Lacking subject matter that conveys tragedy or instills terror, there is no basis for the feeling of the sublime. And if it were possible, he assumes that the experience of the sublime requires the perceiver to feel personally threatened. This is nonsense, of course, since we can experience sublimity in films and other visual media without believing that what is represented is an actual threat. Nonetheless, Schopenhauer concludes that successful music is always beautiful, but it is never sublime. (Alex Neill points out that this position seems inconsistent with Schopenhauer's recognition of the sublime in nature.) As for music, I do not think it necessary to locate a subject matter in Shostakovich's late string quartets in order to experience genuine sublimity—we don't have to respond to them, as is often done, as his musical autobiography. But any theory that cannot recognize the presence or value of sublimity in music without texts or programmatic association is seriously flawed, especially as an account of music's capacity to reveal the ineffable. (In this respect, Schopenhauer's view foreshadows Peter Kivy's recent argument that pure instrumental music cannot be profound, for profound art requires profound subject matter. However, sublimity is an aesthetic property, whereas profundity is not so clearly one. So I will not pursue the topic of profundity any further.)

Luckily, I think that Schopenhauer's account presents us with a pair of false dilemmas. The remainder of this chapter will argue that the presence of concepts and cultural conventions unleashes—rather than reduces—music's capacity to show the ineffable. Specifically, I will make my case by concentrating on the aesthetic property that Schopenhauer does not assign to revelatory music: the sublime. There is a price to pay, however. We cannot suppose that music is the unique route to a revelation of some aspects of the inner nature of the world. I am willing to concede that many representational artworks can do it, too. An obvious example is J.M.W. Turner's *Snow Storm: Steamboat off a Harbour's Mouth* (1842). Another is Caspar David Friedrich's *Das Eismeer* (The Polar Sea, *c.* 1823). Coincidentally, both paintings show the forces of nature overpowering a ship. In each case the ship provides a sense of scale for the forces of nature. Imaginatively attuned viewers can then grasp the sublimity of what is represented, and will grasp the mystical or spiritual dimension of the scene. Although instrumental music does not work on our imaginations in precisely the same way, we can take comfort in Marghanita Laski's finding that a significantly spiritual experience arises twice as often with music than with other art forms. Many of these experiences, which she calls "ecstasy," fit into modern descriptions of the experience of the sublime.

IV. ISN'T IT SUBJECTIVE?

Against those who encounter musical sublimity and interpret it as the siren call of infinity, Mary Mothersill warns, "The sense of spiritual elevation is not an indication of actual spiritual elevation." When that sense of elevation comes by way of sublimity, we face the skeptical challenge that sublimity is utterly subjective. In Kant's words, "sublimity is contained not in anything of nature, but only in our mind." Therefore experiences of sublimity cannot be informative about a spiritual dimension of nature or the universe. This criticism is often buttressed with a dose of materialism. The experience is nothing more than a subjective awareness of some change in one's body chemistry and neurological firing. A classic version of the skeptical response is provided by Ebenezer Scrooge upon the appearance of the ghost of his partner, Jacob Marley. "A slight disorder of the stomach makes them cheats." The sight of a ghost might be caused by something other than a supernatural being. It might have a more worldly explanation: "an undigested bit of beef, a blot of mustard, a crumb of cheese, a fragment of an underdone potato." Substitute musical form for undigested beef, and the skeptic can deny that there is any genuine other-worldly significance in what *seems* to be an experience of the supernatural. Sound waves go into the ear, neural signals go to the brain, and appropriately receptive listeners respond with a sense of something spiritual.

Although I have my own reservations about reading too much into the siren call of music, this brand of explanatory reduction is inadequate. Granted, a material explanation tells us a lot about the process by which we come to have the experience that we have. For example, it explains how the process breaks down for some people. In Chapter 2, I mentioned congenital amusia. I have no doubt that it is due to abnormalities in the operations of the brain. However, it does not follow that there is nothing more to the experience of the ineffable or the divine than a particular brain activity. Knowing how a mobile phone works to produce the sound of my wife's voice does not cancel out the fact that the sounds are highly accurate indications of what she is saying into the speaker of her phone. Analogously, identifying sonic patterns in music that reliably stimulate the brain to produce experiences of awe and of ineffable significance does not cancel out the possibility that something ineffable is conveyed by the music. The Book of Exodus says that God got Moses' attention by setting fire to a bush. Then God spoke from the bush. And why not? In a tradition that holds that individuals are free to attend to God or not, as they choose, it makes sense to think that God will entice attention by creating spectacular occurrences. Where God created a bush that burns but is not consumed, Beethoven and Coltrane offer music. In each case, external stimuli are selected according to their ability to attract and hold attention.

Let's enrich this sketch of an argument by examining visual perception. Science offers a very detailed account of the underlying neurobiological mechanisms. I watch a formation of geese rippling through the sky. In order to see them, the electrical stimulation of my occipital lobe must originate in my optic nerve. For its part, the signal that arises in the optic nerve must be a response to light waves that reach my retina, indicating movement of objects within my visual field. Provided with these facts, does anyone jump to the conclusion that seeing is *nothing but* conscious awareness of stimulation of a particular region of the brain? That there is no further significance to the activation of the occipital lobe? That inference is absurd! Granted, if any of the connections fail, then my *seeming* to see geese will be something other than seeing geese. If my visual experience is not responding to real-time changes in the world beyond my own body, then I am dreaming, or hallucinating. Because visual dreaming also involves electrical activity in the occipital lobe, a vivid dream may look just like the real deal. But that doesn't reduce life to a continuous dream. The difference between "seeing" dream geese and seeing real geese is not simply a matter of what happens in the brain. It matters whether the electrical signals are appropriate responses to activity in the world beyond my retinas. Subjectively, seeing geese and dreaming of geese might be indistinguishable, yet they are very different with respect to their informational significance about the world at the time they occur.

These points about vision apply to hearing, as well. Like the eyes, the ears are pathways to the world. Sound waves are objective events in the world. Replace the optic nerve with the auditory nerve, the retina with specialized hair cells in the cochlea of the inner ear, and the occipital lobe with the region known as Heschl's gyrus. Granted, hearing is not always an indicator that sound waves have tickled the cochlea of the inner ear. As with the occipital lobe, the auditory cortex can generate "hearing" when there is no external stimulus. We can hear sounds in a dream. Many people experience earworms—those snatches of music that keep playing over and over in the head. Years of listening to music at high volumes often cause the phantom sounds of tinnitus—often in the form of a steady buzzing or ringing sound—arising from damage to hair cells in the inner ear. And there are auditory hallucinations, too. But these facts do not override the fact that the auditory system is designed to perceive external, objective relationships.

The next step is to emphasize that our perceptual system is an aesthetically sensitive system. We do not see mere shapes, colors, and movements. Responding to the complex interplay of countless features of what we perceive, our eyes detect an array of aesthetic properties. We see beauty, gracefulness, and delicacy. There are also disagreeable properties, such as ugliness, dumpiness, and garishness. As with other features of human perception, I assume that distinctive brain activity underlies them all, including our sense of awe and of revelation when we view sublime sights or imaginatively interact with representations of them. As neuroscience becomes more sophisticated, I anticipate that we'll identify distinct neuro-biological responses for many different aesthetic responses. I predict that we will verify that there are interesting gender and cultural differences in neurobiological responses to the same art, literature, and music. All of which reinforces the need to explain why humans have a proclivity to experience beauty in rainbows and in other visual data, and why we recognize *so many* different aesthetic properties intertwined with our experiences of the world beyond ourselves.

As before, it's not simply a matter of seeing. We *hear* aesthetic properties, too, as features that emerge from com-binations of sounds. In Richard Wagner's operatic *Ring* cycle, the melodic motif of Fafner the dragon is ungainly. In popular music, many of Nick Drake's songs are delicate. His singing has a fragile quality, giving his performances of them an admirable unity. In contrast, the songs and performances of the Shaggs are clumsy and awkward. Appreciated as moments in a culture's development, musical compositions and performances can also display aesthetic properties with a distinctly historical component. Because his work is largely in film scoring, John Williams is the best-known living orchestral composer. Yet his work is phenomenally derivative. In the late 1920s, the songs of the Carter Family were traditional while the guitar playing of Maybelle Carter was highly original. Her "Carter scratch" also became astoundingly influential. The aesthetic properties of sounding derivative, traditional, and original will be inaudible to someone who approaches the music in a cultural vacuum. Nonetheless, these and other aesthetic properties are a significant element of the experience of music.

Along with the sound patterns that generate them, don't experiences of aesthetic properties convey information about the external world? If they do not, why do humans possess a proclivity to make fine-grained distinctions among so many of them?

V. EXPERIENCING SUBLIMITY

The full list of aesthetic properties is enormous. From the thrill of a roller coaster ride to the stark nobility of many of Mark Rothko's later paintings, it includes any feature of an experience that makes an aesthetic difference. In other words, an aesthetic property is present whenever an element of an experience makes that experience good or bad, better or worse, when we evaluate it simply as an experience. However, "experience" is a broader category than sense perception. Aesthetic properties are also present in experiences that arise in imagination and, occasionally, intellectual thought.

For my purposes, I do not have to offer a detailed account of aesthetic responses and their bases. It will be enough to focus on certain parallels between aesthetic properties and powerful human emotions such as fear, grief, and shame. Given their prominence in perception, it is unlikely that beauty and other paradigm aesthetic properties are merely subjective ephemera. My central proposal is that experiences of aesthetic properties are inherently significant. Like our emotions, they are directed at events and objects in the world. They are ways of regarding the world.

Once again, let's consider an experience of seeing and hearing geese in flight. Their formation ripples gracefully. In comparison, their honking is coarse, bordering on ugly. Gracefulness and ugliness are aesthetic properties that emerge from our awareness of combinations of other properties that we experience. For my purposes, the important issue is whether aesthetic properties reveal something substantive about the world. I noted that many people are subjectivists when it comes to these properties. Another classic formulation is David Hume's pronouncement, "Beauty is no quality in things themselves: It exists merely in the mind which contemplates them." However, even Hume grants that this mental response is not random. The perception of beauty is like seeing color or tasting the sweetness of honey. These three responses are similar in that they all involve sensitivity to objective forms and structures in the objects we perceive. Aesthetic properties emerge from and thus supplement the other properties we experience. The visible movement of the skein of geese tells me that they're heading south. So what does the graceful flow of the skein show me, over and above the fact of movement? At the very least, it immediately conveys their successful group coordination. If I focus on the individual birds, I become aware of their individual athleticism. Each bird continuously beats its wings, its head held steady but its body dragging down as it loses altitude with each up-stroke of wings, then pushing itself up again on the next down-stroke, over and over again. Not very graceful. Taken as a group, however, their gracefulness is like that of an Olympic scull team of eight rowers. The individuals are straining, but the overall effect is lovely. In both cases, the gracefulness is a gestalt property. It is not observed when we shift our attention to the workings of the isolated parts. It is an aesthetic effect of the whole, signifying the highly successful coordination of those parts.

Although aesthetic properties involve an assessment of information about the world, I am not suggesting that experiences of gracefulness and beauty and sublimity require a conscious awareness of this information. In this respect, aesthetic responses are very similar to emotional responses. (Hume goes so far as to say that aesthetic responses are emotions; they are "calm" passions.) Central cases of emotion —anger, lust, fear, grief, joy—are modes of judging one's relationship to the natural and social environment. This is different from saying that these emotions are *caused* by particular thought patterns. Remember my earlier observation that our emotions *are* thoughts: they are judgments that situate us in the world. A sudden feeling of fear is not a response to a perception of danger. The fear is itself a judgment that danger is present, bound up with a physiological response that prepares us to avoid a potential harm. Grief is not a reaction to the judgment that one has suffered a loss so much as it is itself a way of perceiving that there is a significant loss. In each of these cases, Robert Solomon notes, there is an important difference between making the judgment emotionally and then reflecting on it consciously. Granted, an emotion often leads to conscious reflection on its significance. If I feel angry, I generally think I know who I am angry with, and why.

However, this conscious belief is not always correct, or remains obscure. Who has never had an inexplicable pang of fear, seemingly unrelated to any danger that could be consciously identified?

Analogously, experiences of aesthetic properties are judgments about the objects or scenes that incite them. Aesthetic properties can be regarded as subjective in so far as they are experiential aspects of perception and other cognitive processing, and thus mental phenomena. Furthermore, they are easily dismissed as subjective by anyone who holds that all value judgments are subjective. If we perceive a porcelain figurine as dainty and charming, rather than sentimental and cloying, we judge it positively rather than negatively. However, such examples also show that aesthetic judgments are not *purely* evaluative. They are assessments with a descriptive element. Once we move beyond completely generic terms of praise like "good" and "successful," aesthetic terminology provides a degree of description about the object of the judgment. In describing the music of some of Amy Elsie Horrocks's songs as "most dainty and charming," the *Musical News* of 1895 calls attention to very different non-aesthetic features than when praising a religious anthem by another composer as melodious and "bright in character." By extension, when I tell you that Shostakovich's string quartet in C minor (Op. 110) is sublime and Warren Zevon's song "Hasten Down the Wind" has a beautiful melody, I am informing you that they succeed in very different ways. When we praise music by describing it as beautiful or as sublime, we do not employ interchangeable terms of recommendation.

The further analogy with emotion is that the situational details that distinguish musical daintiness from brightness— and beauty from sublimity—are not transparently evident to the perceiver. When people become angry, their conscious belief about the reasons for the anger can involve self-deception or error about its real object. It is not self-evident which of the object's aspects inform the angry response. The same is true of aesthetic judgment. In Peter Kivy's words, "bafflement before the work of art is a common occurrence. How often have we experienced 'unity,' 'balance,' 'rightness,' and the like, and yet been unable to 'put our finger' on the feature or features responsible?" Many people experience the derivativeness of John Williams's music for *Star Wars* without being able to name any specific sources, or they say that it sounds like Richard Wagner when it actually sounds much more like Erich Wolfgang Korngold. Furthermore, reflective judgments about aesthetic responses generally reflect cultural biases. Beethoven, for example, gives a specifically monotheistic interpretation to the experience of natural beauty: "The chance meeting of agreeable atoms did not make the world. If the constitution of the world reflects order and beauty, then God exists." The great challenge, therefore, is locating the basic judgment about the world that is inherent in the experience of each aesthetic experience.

I grant that there are aberrant experiences. Some people hear voices when none are present. Some amputees feel pain in a missing limb. Likewise, some people experience ugliness where almost everyone else finds beauty. But that is no more troubling than recognizing that some people have aberrant emotional responses, too. What we want to understand is *what judgment occurs* as an element of the experience. This task is different from isolating typical external causes. Suppose that certain general musical patterns are present in many of the musical works that reliably generate feelings of the sublime and the associated belief that one is in the presence of something mystical or supernatural. The measured cadence of chant is a candidate. Identifying these patterns is only a small step toward an account of musical sublimity. We also want to know how our orientation to the world changes when we have this response. Anger and fear and other emotions influence human behavior. Does the experience of sublimity, as well?

As I noted earlier, the feeling of the sublime is characterized by awe, astonishment, admiration, and pleasure (even of exhilaration) that accompanies a feeling of being over-whelmed. Sometimes, it mingles with fear or terror or a painful incomprehension. As with other significant feelings, the fact that there is a strong physiological response should not blind us to the fact that the experience of sublimity includes a world-directed judgment. It is the judgment that we are in the presence of something that is simultaneously extraordinary and ineffable. It appears to depend on a sequence of two prefatory judgments. First, there is an immediate judgment of our cognitive disruption. Second, there is recognition of our insignificance in the face of some overwhelming scene or event. The sensory and imaginative disruption of our ordinary relationship to the world prompts, in Malcolm Budd's very nice formulation, "the sudden dropping away . . . of our everyday sense of the importance of our self and its numerous concerns and projects." Typically, the perceiver loses any sense of the distinction between perceiver and perceived. Individuals who make a positive evaluation of the disruptive experience regard it as revelatory. Some individuals do not regard it as positive and it feels confusing, or horrific, or unpleasantly bizarre. Thus a Shostakovich string quartet or an hour-long Grateful Dead improvisation that Deadheads regard as spiritually revelatory can seem merely horrific and boring to the ordinary pop music fan. But if Nica de Koenigswarter experienced sublimity in "'Round Midnight," she may well have heard it as a declaration of freedom.

Contrary to John Keats, I do not believe "Beauty is truth, truth beauty." The evaluative element of an aesthetic response is not truth-functional (i.e., subject to the contrasting values of truth and falsity). A great deal of beautiful art tells beautiful lies. Because aesthetic responses are simultaneously evaluations and beliefs, the aesthetic properties of artworks provide an important standard for success that is not truth-functional. In this context, recall Wittgenstein's point that descriptive language cannot describe the mystical. After all, if ordinary language is adequate, then the mystical is not ineffable. The ineffable and the mystical arise at the point where description ends and where thoughts and communication cannot be evaluated truth-functionally. Success or failure in communicating the experience of the mystical must be measured by other criteria. In some art, this is done through the incorporation of sublimity. A work of fictional literature can contain many true statements, as when Joyce takes great care to provide an accurate description of the railings at 7 Eccles Street, Dublin. However, as Lyotard argues, the sublime element of Ulysses arises from Joyce's employment of allusion, which is quite different from saying that it is an articulated truth within his strings of true propositions. To experience the sublimity of Ulysses, readers must aesthetically savor and positively assess its cumulative ineffability. In music, similarly, a listener's sense of reaching the ineffable is intimately connected with the music's aesthetic success. Mere awareness that the composer is attempting to do so is never sufficient. For those of us who find Arvo Pärt's music boring and insipid, the music lacks sublimity. It promises revelation but disappoints. Genuine communication of the sublime is achieved by providing an experience of sublimity, a proposal that I explain in greater detail in the next section.

Pulling these points together, paradigm experiences of sublimity require an experience of something as limitless, so that it overwhelms our normal ability to make sense of its organization or scope. Ordinarily, such experiences are generated by the presence of something that overwhelms our perceptual and cognitive systems. At night in the wilderness, away from the distractions of artificial light, the sight of the stars in a cloudless night frequently generates a sense of awe. The number of stars and their brightness are both relevant to the experience. These experiences can be replicated in representations, so the same aesthetic effect—and so the same significance—is present in Vincent van Gogh's painting *The Starry Night* (1889). Or, in a less frenetic mode, there is Caspar David Friedrich's *Northern Sea in the Moonlight* (1824). The two paintings have very different styles. Van Gogh overwhelms us. In contrast, Friedrich's composition is nearly formless. Lyotard notes that these two very different approaches to art are inspired by Kant's analysis of the sublime: "a figural aesthetic of the 'much too much' that defies the concept [of genius], and an abstract or minimal aesthetic of the 'almost nothing' that defies form." Musical parallels are Coltrane's performances with Eric Dolphy at the Village Vanguard in 1961, and Philip Glass's music for the film *Koyaanisqatsi*, respectively.

To take stock, several species of aesthetic response have come to be known as the experience of sublimity. One species is a positive response to scenes or events that overwhelm conceptual processing. Because the perceiver is *appreciating* this loss of coherence and attendant loss of sense of self, many details about what seems revelatory about the experience are necessarily ineffable. In this way, sublimity in music adds a layer of ineffability that supplements the normal ineffability of musical experience. Musical sublimity will therefore display both types of ineffability: the first is typical of all music, while the second is a disruptive impact on the sense of self and self importance.

VI. EXEMPLIFICATION

Schopenhauer's account of music is historically important in several ways. He brought non-Western insights into European aesthetics and he gave philosophical support to the idea that music is "an entirely universal language" that reveals the ineffable. More to the point, Schopenhauer highlights the conflict between universality and artifice. His philosophy defends the widespread conviction that music is most powerful when it is not constrained by convention and tradition. Musical revelation eliminates the middle man, so to speak. The music communicates, rather than the composer. It is as if Beethoven did not play the piano: the piano played Beethoven. As a student of mystical philosophy, rock guitarist Robert Fripp has claimed that this position explains the haphazard history of his group, King Crimson: "Music so wishes to be heard that it sometimes calls on unlikely characters to give it voice." The same ideal informed John Cage's adoption of chance procedures as a compositional technique. Coincidentally, and apparently without direct influence on Schopenhauer, this same stance towards music and composers appears in Hoffmann's defense of Beethoven. Hoffmann treats Haydn and Mozart as historical individuals who crafted music to achieve their personal aims. But when the music is shaped by a composer's intentions and training, its capacity to show the mystical disappears behind the veil of musical artifice. With Beethoven's symphonies, the composer is no longer the active agent. Hoffmann says that music opens the door to infinity. The music, not the composer, "opens up to us . . . the realm of the monstrous and the immeasurable." (I owe this observation to Mark Evan Bonds.)

In this section I address this bias against stylistic or conscious interventions of composers and performers as active interpreters of the transcendent. Against this bias, I argue that human intervention is required to impart extra-musical significance to music. Sublime music cannot have an extra-musical reference apart from human use, and therefore it cannot have a revelatory function unless someone offers the music in that spirit. In the last section I argued that awareness of sublimity involves a distinctive judgment about the perceiver's relationship to the sublime object. I will now argue that artistic intervention permits, rather than interferes with, the music's capacity to reveal an ineffable, sublime dimension of extra-musical reality. Music does so through exemplification.

Throughout this book I have argued that music is a dimension of culture. Consequently, any response to it that is not hopelessly superficial is directed by language. So I am in no position to suppose the music's spirituality will be found in a universal, culture-independent capacity of music. Instead, I propose that music's ability to communicate the ineffable does not disappear if the experience is mediated by cultural conventions, conceptual thought, and artistic intervention. The Book of Revelation of the Christian New Testament is written in Koine Greek, and the Qur'an is written in a particular Arabic dialect. By itself, the fact of their having been encoded in a convention-based language counts neither for nor against their legitimacy as spiritual revelation. Similarly, the fact that Coltrane's *A Love Supreme* displays a post-bop, free jazz style counts neither for nor against its capacity to convey spiritual truth. Instead, we should acknowledge that the presence of musical conventions enables composers and performers to introduce musical elements that will guide the aesthetic responses of their listeners. Sublimity is one such response.

Contrary to the tradition endorsed by Hoffmann, Schopenhauer, and so many others, let us suppose that Beethoven *intended* to create sublime music when he composed his seventh symphony. Suppose that the Adagio of Anton Bruckner's eighth symphony and some Coltrane improvisations are sublime *by design*. Incidentally, I do not think that the relevant intention has to be the authorial intention of a lone individual. There are also group intentions, as when the Coltrane quartet works together to perform "Chasin' the Train" and works cooperatively to make it sublime. When music is sublime by design, that feature of the music can be more than an instance of the general aesthetic property of sublimity. It can also serve as an exemplification of that property, thereby showing by direct example that there is an available path to the mystical. The plausibility of this argument depends on a distinction between being an instance of something, representing it, and exemplifying it.

As I have done repeatedly, I will begin with a visual example. The property of greenness is instantiated by many things: ripe Granny Smith apples, the jerseys worn by the Green Bay Packers for "home" games, and Kermit the Frog. Suppose I have a reason to determine which of these shades of green is darkest. However, I do not have a Green Bay jersey at hand and cannot recall whether its characteristic green is darker or lighter than Kermit. I search the Internet for color photographs of each thing. These photographs *represent* the objects that interest me. As representations, the photographs direct me to extra-pictorial things while offering limited information about them. Trusting that the shades of green in the photos approximate those of the represented objects, I can determine that Kermit is a lighter shade of green than the jerseys. However, while this method succeeds in this case, representations often mislead us or lack the information we seek. Many visual representations do not show the color of the represented object. Suppose that I locate a chalk and pastel drawing of Kermit wearing a Green Bay jersey, but the drawing is executed with the same color palette used by James McNeill Whistler for his *Nocturne, San Giorgio* (1880). Although the orange and brown colors will represent both Kermit and the jersey, the drawing does not employ green and it does not offer any clue about whether Kermit or the jersey has the darker shade of green. Silly as it is, this example illustrates why only a naïve viewer will believe that an object shown in a representation has the very same properties that the representation possesses. And it is not simply a problem of omission, as when the drawing of green things omits greenness. Representations frequently add properties to things that are not their genuine properties. For example, Paul Revere's print of the Boston Massacre of 1770 clearly shows Captain Thomas Preston with a raised sword, which represents Preston as commanding his troops to fire on the unarmed civilians. Preston did no such thing. For expressive purposes, Henri Matisse runs a green stripe down the face of his wife in the portrait of 1905.

What about *aesthetic properties* of representational art? Once again, a representation's aesthetic properties may or may not match the aesthetic properties of whatever it represents. For example, there is a long tradition in Western thought that praises art for its capacity to beautify nature. When Charles Batteux offers the first philosophically complete definition of art, in 1746, he defines "les beaux arts" as human products that beautifully imitate nature. No matter what the reality is, artists should beautify what they represent. Consequently, paintings executed within this tradition are not reliable guides to the degree of beauty that is really present in their subject matter. To put it crudely, cautious viewers will understand that the aesthetic property of beauty may be imposed as part of the artistic process. Today, we see a similar tendency in the practice of manipulating photographs in advertising, digitally changing the proportions of women to make them more attractive. Furthermore, beauty is not the only property at issue. Consider the use of "body doubles" in filmmaking. In *Flashdance* (1983), many close shots of the dancing of the character of Alex show someone other than lead actress Jennifer Beals. By editing together the dancing of two different women, Alex's dancing displays aesthetic properties that Beals could not achieve.

Generalizing, Schopenhauer seems to have a point. A musical representation is completely untrustworthy. Fortunately, representation is not the only method of symbolization available to artists and composers. Nelson Goodman has taken pains to remind us about exemplification, in which one object that provides an instance of a property or group of properties is intentionally offered as a *sample* of the property or properties.

The practice of exemplification is not restricted to art. When I want to purchase new wall-to-wall carpets for a room, I go to the flooring store and look at carpet samples. The samples share relevant properties with the big rolls of carpet that are stored in the warehouse. By examining the samples, I can directly experience properties that are not adequately conveyed through representation. The samples exemplify what I can purchase. However, not all of a sample's properties enter into the exemplification relationship. When I look at the sample in the showroom and turn it over, I find a label that says, "Do not Remove. Property of Jones Brothers Flooring." However, I do not take this to mean that any carpeting that I purchase will have to remain in the showroom as their property. As with every exemplification, the sample refers the informed user to some, but not all, of its properties. The intended use of a sample plays an indispensable role in demarcating some properties as exemplified when others are not. Successful exemplification always requires an understanding of shared purposes.

The upshot of this account of exemplification is that an artwork can be used to exemplify particular aesthetic properties, thereby *showing* the aesthetic properties of something other than itself. This power to show is not reduced by intrusion of musical culture, as Schopenhauer fears. Musical exemplification is not secured by appeal to music's status as a universal language. There is no symbolization through exemplification without the direction of culture. For example, the sublimity of St Peter's Basilica is designed to exemplify the sublimity of the church (the earthly institution) and of God. Likewise, the adagio of Bruckner's eighth symphony and certain Coltrane improvisations create sublime experiences in knowledgeable listeners by exploiting shared musical expectations. On a sympathetic reading of what Bruckner and Coltrane were doing, their music successfully exemplifies a relationship with extra-musical reality. If I am mistaken and Bruckner and Coltrane intended nothing of the kind when they made sublimity a prominent feature of their music, then their music possesses sublimity without exemplifying sublimity.

By providing listeners with an opportunity to experience musical sublimity that exemplifies non-musical sublimity, composers show without saying. They show listeners that they can enter into an ineffable relationship with revelatory potential.

Michael Mitias aims two objections at this theory of exemplification. First, artworks do not literally possess sublimity, so they cannot exemplify it. Second, aesthetic responses to art are always uniquely colored by the particularity of the artwork. Therefore they cannot be trusted to be accurate examples of the same property in anything else. Applied to Bruckner or Coltrane, the argument is that the music is not sublime and so cannot exemplify sublimity, and to the extent that they prompt a sublime response, Bruckner's music and Coltrane's music structure the listener's experience in very different ways. Beyond the fact that each listener has a different subjective response in each case of hearing music, musical differentiation guarantees that music does not provide the same experience that is found to be revelatory in an extra-musical experience.

These objections are not convincing. Strictly speaking, aesthetic properties are aspects of mental responses, and on this basis we might concede that music is not literally sublime or beautiful. However, this concession is no more troubling than saying a green carpet sample is not literally green or brown, because the visual properties of greenness and brownness are subjective human responses. It doesn't render visual experiences of color meaningless on a global scale. Objections have to be launched on a case-by-case basis, by detailing a concern about whether there is a connection to external stimuli. The same holds, I have argued, for the significance of experiences of ineffability and loss of self. It is the *experience*, strictly speaking, that is exemplified by the practice of creating sublime music in a context that invites listeners to understand it as a "sample" of the mystical side of extra-musical reality. We should question the musical competence of someone who thinks that the song "The Rain in Spain" in *My Fair Lady* (1964) is sublime, but not someone who knows Romantic music and says so about a Bruckner adagio.

The second objection also fails. Samples work by having some properties that they share with something else. To worry us regarding music, Matias's objection would have to show that exemplification never succeeds. For purposes of this argument, let us assume that Roman Catholicism is the one true faith. Yet no one of that faith supposes that the sublime experience offered by St Peter's Basilica is identical to the sublimity of God on the Day of Judgment. But so what? Every square inch of carpet in the carpet warehouse is unique in some way, too, but that doesn't prevent the carpet dealer from showing functional samples to the customers. The point of a sample is that it offers a focused, limited experience in situations where it is not practical or not possible to have more. In principle, there is no reason why the experience of sublime music cannot offer us a genuine sample of the realm that Wittgenstein summarizes as "the mystical." Individuals may interpret it as an experience of God, or the Universal Will, or something else, but that interpretation is not inherent in the experience.

In conclusion, I emphasize that my proposal is limited to communication of the ineffable involving musical sublimity. I have argued that some music provides a sublime experience, which of necessity involves a positive appreciation of an ineffable experience that both supplements ordinary musical ineffability and contains some degree of revelation, typically about human insignificance. When music provides a sublime experience in a tradition that encourages exemplification of the sublime, as has been the case in Europe during and following the Romantic period, the music makes a non-representational reference beyond itself. Through exemplification, different styles of classical music, jazz, and even popular music can be employed to induce experiences of the sublime that exemplify and thus confirm a more general human capacity for ineffable encounters with the mystical. Claims about music's capacity to reveal the mystical are not without merit.

References

Adorno, Theodor, *Essays on Music*, ed. R. Leppert, Berkeley, University of California Press, 2002.

——, *Aesthetic Theory*, ed. G. Adorno and R. Tiedemann, trans. Robert Hullot-Kentor, Minneapolis, University of Minnesota Press, 1997.

Alperson, Philip, "Schopenhauer and Musical Revelation," *Journal of Aesthetics and Art Criticism*, 40, 1981, pp. 155–166.

Augustine, *Enarrationes in Psalmos*, Vol. 1, eds Eligius Dekkers and John Fraipont, Turnhout, Brepols, 1956.

Barzun, Jacques, "Is Music Unspeakable?" *The American Scholar*, 65, 1996, pp. 193–202.

Batteux, Charles, *Les Beaux-arts réduits à un même principe*, Vol. 2 of *Collection Théorie et critique à l'âge classique*, ed. Jean-Rémy Mantion, Paris, Aux Amateurs de Livres, 1989.

Beethoven, Ludwig van, *Beethoven im eigenen Wort*, ed. Friedrich Kerst, Berlin, Schuster & Loeffler, 1904.

Bell, Clive, *Art*, London, Chatto & Windus, 1914.

Benamou, Marc, *Rasa: Affect and Intuition in Javanese Musical Aesthetics* (AMS Studies in Music), New York, Oxford University Press, 2010.

Bicknell, Jeanette, *Why Music Moves Us*, New York, Palgrave Macmillan, 2009.

Boethius, Anicius Manlius Severinus, *Fundamentals of Music* [*De institutione musica*], trans. Calvin M. Bower, New Haven, Yale University Press, 1989.

Bonds, Mark Evan, *Music as Thought: Listening to the Symphony in the Age of Beethoven*, Princeton, Princeton University Press, 2006.

Bruhn, Siglind (ed.), *Voicing the Ineffable: Musical Representations of Religious Experience*, Hillsdale, Pendragon Press, 2002.

Budd, Malcolm, *The Aesthetic Appreciation of Nature: Essays on the Aesthetics of Nature*, New York, Oxford University Press, 2002.

——, "Music as an Abstract Art," in *Values of Art: Pictures, Poetry and Music*, London, Penguin Press, 1995, pp. 124–171.

Carroll, Noël, "Notes on Movie Music," in *Theorizing the Moving Image*, Cambridge, University of Cambridge Press, 1996, pp. 139–145.

Catherine of Siena, *The Dialogue*, trans. Suzanne Noffke, New York, Paulist Press, 1980.

Chua, Daniel K.L., *Absolute Music and the Construction of Meaning*, Cambridge, Cambridge University Press, 1999.

Cobussen, Marcel, *Thresholds: Rethinking Spirituality through Music*, Aldershot, Ashgate, 2008.

Confucius, *The Analects*, trans. and ed. D.C. Lau, New York, Penguin Books, 1979.

Coomaraswamy, Ananda Kentish, *The Dance of Siva: Fourteen Indian Essays*, New York, Sunwise Turn, 1918.

Cross, Craig, *The Beatles: Day-By-Day, Song-By-Song, Record-By-Record*, Lincoln, iUniverse, 2005.

Crowther, Paul, *Defining Art, Creating the Canon: Artistic Value in an Era of Doubt*, Oxford, Clarendon Press, 2007.

——, *The Kantian Sublime: From Morality to Art*, Oxford, Oxford University Press, 1986.

Currey, Josiah Seymour, *Abraham Lincoln's Visit to Evanston in 1860*, Evanston, City National Bank, 1914.

Currie, Gregory, "Art for Art's Sake in the Old Stone Age," *Postgraduate Journal of Aesthetics*, 6, 2009, pp. 1–23.

Davies, Stephen, *Musical Understandings and Other Essays on the Philosophy of Music*, Oxford, Oxford University Press, 2011.

Delamain, Jacques, *Why Birds Sing*, trans. Ruth Sarason and Anna Sarason, New York, Coward-McCann, 1931.

Derrida, Jacques, *Acts of Religion*, ed. Gil Anidjar, New York, Routledge, 2002.

Dickens, Charles, *A Christmas Carol: In Prose: Being a Ghost Story of Christmas*, London, Chapman & Hall, 1843.

Dissanayake, Ellen, *What is Art For?*, Seattle, University of Washington Press, 1988.

Dreyfus, Hubert L., *On the Internet*, London and New York, Routledge, 2001.

Dutton, Denis, "But They Don't Have Our Concept of Art," *The Art Instinct: Beauty, Pleasure, and Human Evolution*, Oxford, Oxford University Press, 2009, pp. 64–84.

Elson, Louis Charles, *Shakespeare in Music: A Collation of the Chief Musical Allusions in the Plays of Shakespeare*, Boston, L.C. Page, 1900.

Everett, Walter, *The Beatles as Musicians: Revolver Through the Anthology*, New York, Oxford University Press, 1999.

Feld, Steven, *Sound and Sentiment: Birds, Weeping, Poetics, and Song in Kaluli Expression*, Philadelphia, University of Pennsylvania Press, 1982.

Fergusson, Robert, *The Works of Robert Fergusson*, Edinburgh, Abernethy & Walker, 1805.

Fink, Robert, *Repeating Ourselves: American Minimal Music as Cultural Practice*, Berkeley, University of California Press, 2005.

Gell, Alfred, "The Technology of Enchantment and the Enchantment of Technology," in *Anthropology, Art and Aesthetics*, eds Jeremy Coote and Anthony Shelton, Oxford, Oxford University Press, 1992, pp. 40–66.

Gioia, Ted, *The Imperfect Art: Reflections on Jazz and Modern Culture*, New York, Oxford University Press, 1988.

Goldie, Peter, "Emotion, Feeling, and Knowledge of the World," in *Thinking about Feeling: Contemporary Philosophers on Emotions*, ed. Robert C. Solomon, Oxford, Oxford University Press, 2003, pp. 91–106.

Goodman, Nelson, "How Buildings Mean," *Critical Inquiry*, 11, 1985, pp. 642–653.

Gracyk, Theodore, "The Sublime and the Fine Arts," in *The Sublime: From Antiquity to the Present*, ed. Timothy M. Costelloe, Cambridge, Cambridge University Press, 2012, pp. 217–229.

——, "Music's Worldly Uses," in *Arguing about Art: Contemporary Philosophical Debates*, eds Alex Neill and Aaron Ridley, 3rd ed., London and New York, Routledge, 2007, pp. 135–148.

Guido of Arezzo, *Guido D'Arezzo's Regule rithmice, Prologus in antiphonarium, and Epistola ad michahelem: A Critical Text and Translation*, ed. and trans. Dolores Pesce, Ottawa, Institute of Mediaeval Music, 1999.

Hamilton, Andy, *Aesthetics and Music*, London and New York, Continuum, 2007.

Hanslick, Eduard, *On the Musically Beautiful*, trans. Geoffrey Payzant, Indianapolis, Hackett, 1986.

Hardy, Thomas, *Far from the Madding Crowd*, London, Smith, Elder, & Co., 1874.

Hart, Mickey with Stephen Jay, *Drumming at the Edge of Magic: A Journey into the Spirit of Percussion*, San Francisco, HarperCollins, 1990.

Heine, Heinrich, *Heine's Poems*, ed. Carl Edgar Eggert, Boston, Ginn & Company, 1906.

Hesiod, *Works and Days*, trans. David W. Tandy and Walter C. Neale, Berkeley, University of California Press, 1996.

Higgins, Kathleen, *The Music between Us: Is Music a Universal Language?* Chicago, University of Chicago Press, 2012.

——, "Refined Emotion in Aesthetic Experience: A Cross-Cultural Comparison," in *Aesthetic Experience*, eds Richard M. Shusterman and Adele Tomlin, New York, Routledge, 2008, pp. 106–126.

Hill, Peter and Nigel Simeone, *Olivier Messiaen: Oiseaux exotiques*, Aldershot, Ashgate, 2007.

Hoffmann, E.T.A., "Beethoven's Instrumental Music," trans. William Oliver Strunk, in *Source Readings in Music History* rev. ed., eds William Oliver Strunk and Leo Treitler, New York, W.W. Norton, 1998, pp. 1193–1198.

Homer, *The Odyssey*, trans. Robert Fagles, New York, Penguin, 1996.

Hume, David, *Selected Essays*, eds Stephen Copley and Andrew Edgar, Oxford, Oxford University Press, 1993.

James, William, *The Varieties of Religious Experience: A Study in Human Nature*, The Works of William James, Vol. 15, eds Frederick H. Burkhardt, Fredson Bowers, and Ignas K. Skrupskelis, Cambridge, Harvard University Press, 1985.

Kania, Andrew, "Definition," in *The Routledge Companion to Philosophy and Music*, eds Theodore Gracyk and Andrew Kania, London and New York, Routledge, 2011, pp. 3–13.

Kant, Immanuel, *Critique of Judgment*, trans. Werner S. Pluhar, Indianapolis, Hackett, 1987.

Karnes, Kevin C., *Music, Criticism, and the Challenge of History: Shaping Modern Musical Thought in Late-Nineteenth-Century Vienna*, New York, Oxford University Press, 2008.

Kastin, David, *Nica's Dream: The Life and Legend of the Jazz Baroness*, New York, W.W. Norton, 2011.

Kennedy, Michael, *The Oxford Dictionary of Music*, Oxford, Oxford University Press, 1985.

Kivy, Peter, *Music, Language, and Cognition*, Oxford, Clarendon Press, 2007.

——, *Music Alone: Philosophical Reflections on the Purely Musical Experience*, Ithaca, Cornell University Press, 1990.

——, "Aesthetic Aspects and Aesthetic Qualities," *The Journal of Philosophy*, 65, 1968, pp. 85–93.

Kubler, George, *The Shape of Time*, New Haven, Yale University Press, 1962.

Kumar, Raj, *Essays on Indian Music*, New Delhi, Discovery Publishing, 2003.

Larkin, Philip, *All What Jazz: A Record Diary, 1961–68*, New York, St Martin's Press, 1970.

Laski, Marghanita, *Ecstasy: A Study of Some Secular and Religious Experiences*, New York, Greenwood Press, 1976.

Leach, Elizabeth Eva, *Sung Birds: Music, Nature, and Poetry in the Later Middle Ages*, Ithaca, Cornell University Press, 2007.

Lebrecht, Norman, *The Life and Death of Classical Music: Featuring the 100 Best and 20 Worst Recordings Ever Made*, New York, Anchor Books, 2007.

Lesser, Wendy, *Music for Silenced Voices: Shostakovich and His Fifteen Quartets*, New Haven, Yale University Press, 2011.

Levinson, Jerrold, *Music in the Moment*, Ithaca: Cornell University Press, 1997.

Levitin, Daniel J., *This Is Your Brain on Music: The Science of a Human Obsession*, New York, Penguin, 2006.

Lyotard, Jean-François, *Lessons on the Analytic of the Sublime: Kant's Critique of Judgment*, trans. Elizabeth Rottenberg, Stanford, Stanford University Press, 1994.

——, *The Postmodern Condition: A Report on Knowledge*, trans. Geoff Bennington and Brian Massumi, Minneapolis, University of Minnesota Press, 1984.

McFee, Graham, "Meaning and the Art-Status of 'Music Alone,'" *British Journal of Aesthetics*, 37, 1997, pp. 31–46.

Mersenne, Marin, *Harmonie Universelle, contenant la théorie et la pratique de la musique*, Paris, Cramoisy, 1636.

Mitias, Michael H., *Philosophy and Architecture*, Amsterdam, Rodopi, 1994.

Mothersill, Mary, "Sublime," in *A Companion to Aesthetics*, 2nd ed., eds David Cooper, Stephen Davies, Kathleen Higgins, Robert Hopkins and Robert Stecker, Oxford, Wiley-Blackwell, 2009, pp. 547–551.

Neill, Alex, "Schopenhauer on Tragedy and the Sublime," in *A Companion to Schopenhauer*, ed. Bart Vandenabeele, Malden, Wiley-Blackwell, 2012, pp. 206–218.

Neill, Alex and Aaron Ridley, "Religious Music for Godless Ears," *Mind* 119, 2010, pp. 999–1023.

Nietzsche, Friedrich, *Twilight of the Idols, or, How to Philosophize with a Hammer*, trans. Richard Polt, Indianapolis, Hackett, 1997.

Plato, *Plato: Complete Works*, ed. John M. Cooper, Indianapolis, Hackett Publishing, 1997.

Prinz, Jesse J., *Gut Reactions: A Perceptual Theory of Emotion*, New York, Oxford University Press, 2004.

Rameau, Jean Philippe, *The Complete Theoretical Writings*, Vol. 1, ed. Erwin R. Jacobi, Rome, American Institute of Musicology, 1967.

Ratliff, Ben, *Coltrane: The Story of a Sound*, New York, Picador, 2007.

"Reviews," *Musical News*, 9, 1895, pp. 278–279.

Robinson, Jenefer, *Deeper than Reason: Emotion and its Role in Literature, Music, and Art*, New York, Oxford University Press, 2007.

Rognoni, Luigi, *Gioacchino Rossini*, Turin, ERI, 1968.

Rothenberg, David, *Why Do Birds Sing? A Journey into the Mystery of Birdsong*, New York, Basic Books, 2006.

Rousseau, Jean-Jacques, *Basic Political Writings*, trans. Donald A. Cress, Indianapolis, Hackett Publishing, 1987.

Sacks, Oliver, *Musicophilia; Tales of Music and the Brain*, New York, Alfred A. Knopf, 2007.

Schiller, Friedrich von, *Naive and Sentimental Poetry, and On the Sublime*, trans. Julius A. Elias, New York, Ungar, 1967.

Schopenhauer, Arthur, *The World as Will and Representation*, 2 vols, trans. Eric F.J. Payne, New York, Dover, 1969.

Sengupta, Pradip Kumar, *Foundations of Indian Musicology* (Perspectives in the Philosophy of Art and Culture), New Delhi, Abhinav, 1991.

Senner, Wayne M., Robin Wallace, and William Rhea Meredith (eds), *The Critical Reception of Beethoven's Compositions by His German Contemporaries*, Vol. 2, Lincoln and London, University of Nebraska Press, 2001.

Shankar, Ravi, *My Music, My Life*, New York, Simon & Schuster, 1968.

Siblin, Eric, *The Cello Suites: J.S. Bach, Pablo Casals, and the Search for a Baroque Masterpiece*, New York, Atlantic Monthly/Grove, 2009.

Solomon, Robert C., *The Passions: Emotions and the Meaning of Life*, New York, Doubleday, 1976.

Steiner, Rudolf, *The Inner Nature of Music and the Experience of Tone: Selected Lectures from the Work of Rudolf Steiner*, Spring Valley, N.Y., Anthroposophic Press, 1983.

Tamm, Eric, *Robert Fripp: From King Crimson to Guitar Craft*, London, Faber & Faber, 1990.

Taruskin, Richard, *Music in the Seventeenth and Eighteenth Centuries: The Oxford History of Western Music*, Oxford, Oxford University Press, 2010.

Taylor, Deems, *Walt Disney's Fantasia*, New York, Simon & Schuster, 1940.

Thom, Paul, *For an Audience: A Philosophy of the Performing Arts*, Philadelphia, Temple University Press, 1993.

Tormey, Alan, *The Concept of Expression: A Study in Philosophical Psychology and Aesthetics*, Princeton, Princeton University Press, 1971.

Tudge, Colin, *The Secret Life of Birds: Who They Are and What They Do*, New York, Penguin, 2008.

Tufail, Ibn (Abu Bakr ibn al-Tufail), *The Improvement of Human Reason, Exhibited in the Life of Hai Ebn Yokdhan*, trans. Simon Ockley, London, Powell & Morphew, 1708.

Twain, Mark, *The Autobiography of Mark Twain*, ed. Harriet Elinor Smith, Vol. 1, Berkeley, University of California Press, 2010.

Van der Merwe, Peter, *Roots of the Classical: The Popular Origins of Western Music*, New York, Oxford University Press, 2005.

Wagner, Richard, *Wagner on Music and Drama: A Compendium of Richard Wagner's Prose Works*, eds Albert Goldman and Evert Sprinchorn, New York, E.P. Dutton, 1964; reprinted New York, Da Capo, 1981.

Waldman, Diane, *Mark Rothko, 1903–1970: A Retrospective*, New York, Henry N. Abrams, 1978.

Walton, Kendall L., "Categories of Art," *The Philosophical Review*, 79, 1970, pp. 334–367.

Wenner, Jann S., *Lennon Remembers*, New York, Verso, 2000.

Williams, Peter, "BWV565: A Toccata in D minor for Organ by J. S. Bach?," *Early Music*, 9, July 1981, pp. 330–337.

Wittgenstein, Ludwig, *Philosophical Investigations*, trans. G.E.M. Anscombe, Oxford, Basil Blackwell, 1953.

Wolff, Robert Paul, *The Ideal of the University*, Boston, Beacon, 1969.

Wurth, Kiene Brillenburg, *Musically Sublime: Indeterminacy, Infinity, Irresolvability*, New York, Fordham University Press, 2009.

Yrizarry, Nathan, et al., "Culture and Emotion," in *Cross-Cultural Topics in Psychology*, eds Leonore Loeb Adler and Uwe Peter Gielen, Westport, Praeger, 2001, 2nd ed., pp. 131–147.

Zappa, Frank with Peter Occhiogrosso, *The Real Frank Zappa Book*, New York, Poseidon, 1989.

Index